C-2682   CAREER EXAMINATION SERIES

This is your
PASSBOOK for...

Supervising Bookkeeper

Test Preparation Study Guide
Questions & Answers

NATIONAL LEARNING CORPORATION®

COPYRIGHT NOTICE

This book is SOLELY intended for, is sold ONLY to, and its use is RESTRICTED to individual, bona fide applicants or candidates who qualify by virtue of having seriously filed applications for appropriate license, certificate, professional and/or promotional advancement, higher school matriculation, scholarship, or other legitimate requirements of education and/or governmental authorities.

This book is NOT intended for use, class instruction, tutoring, training, duplication, copying, reprinting, excerption, or adaptation, etc., by:

1) Other publishers
2) Proprietors and/or Instructors of "Coaching" and/or Preparatory Courses
3) Personnel and/or Training Divisions of commercial, industrial, and governmental organizations
4) Schools, colleges, or universities and/or their departments and staffs, including teachers and other personnel
5) Testing Agencies or Bureaus
6) Study groups which seek by the purchase of a single volume to copy and/or duplicate and/or adapt this material for use by the group as a whole without having purchased individual volumes for each of the members of the group
7) Et al.

Such persons would be in violation of appropriate Federal and State statutes.

PROVISION OF LICENSING AGREEMENTS – Recognized educational, commercial, industrial, and governmental institutions and organizations, and others legitimately engaged in educational pursuits, including training, testing, and measurement activities, may address request for a licensing agreement to the copyright owners, who will determine whether, and under what conditions, including fees and charges, the materials in this book may be used them. In other words, a licensing facility exists for the legitimate use of the material in this book on other than an individual basis. However, it is asseverated and affirmed here that the material in this book CANNOT be used without the receipt of the express permission of such a licensing agreement from the Publishers. Inquiries re licensing should be addressed to the company, attention rights and permissions department.

All rights reserved, including the right of reproduction in whole or in part, in any form or by any means, electronic or mechanical, including photocopying, recording, or by any information storage and retrieval system, without permission in writing from the Publisher.

Copyright © 2025 by

National Learning Corporation

212 Michael Drive, Syosset, NY 11791
(516) 921-8888 • www.passbooks.com
E-mail: info@passbooks.com

PASSBOOK® SERIES

THE *PASSBOOK® SERIES* has been created to prepare applicants and candidates for the ultimate academic battlefield – the examination room.

At some time in our lives, each and every one of us may be required to take an examination – for validation, matriculation, admission, qualification, registration, certification, or licensure.

Based on the assumption that every applicant or candidate has met the basic formal educational standards, has taken the required number of courses, and read the necessary texts, the *PASSBOOK® SERIES* furnishes the one special preparation which may assure passing with confidence, instead of failing with insecurity. Examination questions – together with answers – are furnished as the basic vehicle for study so that the mysteries of the examination and its compounding difficulties may be eliminated or diminished by a sure method.

This book is meant to help you pass your examination provided that you qualify and are serious in your objective.

The entire field is reviewed through the huge store of content information which is succinctly presented through a provocative and challenging approach – the question-and-answer method.

A climate of success is established by furnishing the correct answers at the end of each test.

You soon learn to recognize types of questions, forms of questions, and patterns of questioning. You may even begin to anticipate expected outcomes.

You perceive that many questions are repeated or adapted so that you can gain acute insights, which may enable you to score many sure points.

You learn how to confront new questions, or types of questions, and to attack them confidently and work out the correct answers.

You note objectives and emphases, and recognize pitfalls and dangers, so that you may make positive educational adjustments.

Moreover, you are kept fully informed in relation to new concepts, methods, practices, and directions in the field.

You discover that you are actually taking the examination all the time: you are preparing for the examination by "taking" an examination, not by reading extraneous and/or supererogatory textbooks.

In short, this PASSBOOK®, used directedly, should be an important factor in helping you to pass your test.

SUPERVISING BOOKKEEPER

DUTIES:
Under general supervision, with some latitude for independent or unreviewed action or decision, performs computations and clerical work of above average difficulty and responsibility related to financial records; performs related work.

EXAMPLES OF TYPICAL TASKS:
Performs computations and posts or compiles financial data, as directed, for accounting or tax purposes, or for calculating retirement allowances, balances, loans, or refunds. Keeps general ledgers and controlling accounts or subsidiary records used in accounting. Balances or adjusts accounts. Makes journal entries or entries in registers. Assists in processing invoices, vouchers, payrolls, fee collection reports, or applications for retirement allowances, loans, transfers, and refunds. Writes purchase orders, statements, or bills. Answers inquiries over phone. Keeps records and makes reports as required.

SUBJECT OF EXAMINATION:
The written test will be designed to test for knowledge, skills, and or abilities in such areas as:
1. Arithmetic computations including problems involving ability to understand basic bookkeeping principles;
2. Clerical accuracy;
3. Reading comprehension;
4. Chart and table interpretation;
5. Coding;
6. Alphabetic and numeric filing; and
7. Supervision.

HOW TO TAKE A TEST

I. YOU MUST PASS AN EXAMINATION

A. *WHAT EVERY CANDIDATE SHOULD KNOW*

Examination applicants often ask us for help in preparing for the written test. What can I study in advance? What kinds of questions will be asked? How will the test be given? How will the papers be graded?

As an applicant for a civil service examination, you may be wondering about some of these things. Our purpose here is to suggest effective methods of advance study and to describe civil service examinations.

Your chances for success on this examination can be increased if you know how to prepare. Those "pre-examination jitters" can be reduced if you know what to expect. You can even experience an adventure in good citizenship if you know why civil service exams are given.

B. *WHY ARE CIVIL SERVICE EXAMINATIONS GIVEN?*

Civil service examinations are important to you in two ways. As a citizen, you want public jobs filled by employees who know how to do their work. As a job seeker, you want a fair chance to compete for that job on an equal footing with other candidates. The best-known means of accomplishing this two-fold goal is the competitive examination.

Exams are widely publicized throughout the nation. They may be administered for jobs in federal, state, city, municipal, town or village governments or agencies.

Any citizen may apply, with some limitations, such as the age or residence of applicants. Your experience and education may be reviewed to see whether you meet the requirements for the particular examination. When these requirements exist, they are reasonable and applied consistently to all applicants. Thus, a competitive examination may cause you some uneasiness now, but it is your privilege and safeguard.

C. *HOW ARE CIVIL SERVICE EXAMS DEVELOPED?*

Examinations are carefully written by trained technicians who are specialists in the field known as "psychological measurement," in consultation with recognized authorities in the field of work that the test will cover. These experts recommend the subject matter areas or skills to be tested; only those knowledges or skills important to your success on the job are included. The most reliable books and source materials available are used as references. Together, the experts and technicians judge the difficulty level of the questions.

Test technicians know how to phrase questions so that the problem is clearly stated. Their ethics do not permit "trick" or "catch" questions. Questions may have been tried out on sample groups, or subjected to statistical analysis, to determine their usefulness.

Written tests are often used in combination with performance tests, ratings of training and experience, and oral interviews. All of these measures combine to form the best-known means of finding the right person for the right job.

II. HOW TO PASS THE WRITTEN TEST

A. NATURE OF THE EXAMINATION

To prepare intelligently for civil service examinations, you should know how they differ from school examinations you have taken. In school you were assigned certain definite pages to read or subjects to cover. The examination questions were quite detailed and usually emphasized memory. Civil service exams, on the other hand, try to discover your present ability to perform the duties of a position, plus your potentiality to learn these duties. In other words, a civil service exam attempts to predict how successful you will be. Questions cover such a broad area that they cannot be as minute and detailed as school exam questions.

In the public service similar kinds of work, or positions, are grouped together in one "class." This process is known as *position-classification*. All the positions in a class are paid according to the salary range for that class. One class title covers all of these positions, and they are all tested by the same examination.

B. FOUR BASIC STEPS

1) Study the announcement

How, then, can you know what subjects to study? Our best answer is: "Learn as much as possible about the class of positions for which you've applied." The exam will test the knowledge, skills and abilities needed to do the work.

Your most valuable source of information about the position you want is the official exam announcement. This announcement lists the training and experience qualifications. Check these standards and apply only if you come reasonably close to meeting them.

The brief description of the position in the examination announcement offers some clues to the subjects which will be tested. Think about the job itself. Review the duties in your mind. Can you perform them, or are there some in which you are rusty? Fill in the blank spots in your preparation.

Many jurisdictions preview the written test in the exam announcement by including a section called "Knowledge and Abilities Required," "Scope of the Examination," or some similar heading. Here you will find out specifically what fields will be tested.

2) Review your own background

Once you learn in general what the position is all about, and what you need to know to do the work, ask yourself which subjects you already know fairly well and which need improvement. You may wonder whether to concentrate on improving your strong areas or on building some background in your fields of weakness. When the announcement has specified "some knowledge" or "considerable knowledge," or has used adjectives like "beginning principles of…" or "advanced … methods," you can get a clue as to the number and difficulty of questions to be asked in any given field. More questions, and hence broader coverage, would be included for those subjects which are more important in the work. Now weigh your strengths and weaknesses against the job requirements and prepare accordingly.

3) Determine the level of the position

Another way to tell how intensively you should prepare is to understand the level of the job for which you are applying. Is it the entering level? In other words, is this the position in which beginners in a field of work are hired? Or is it an intermediate or advanced level? Sometimes this is indicated by such words as "Junior" or "Senior" in the class title. Other jurisdictions use Roman numerals to designate the level – Clerk I, Clerk II, for example. The word "Supervisor" sometimes appears in the title. If the level is not indicated by the title, check the description of duties. Will you be working under very close supervision, or will you have responsibility for independent decisions in this work?

4) Choose appropriate study materials

Now that you know the subjects to be examined and the relative amount of each subject to be covered, you can choose suitable study materials. For beginning level jobs, or even advanced ones, if you have a pronounced weakness in some aspect of your training, read a modern, standard textbook in that field. Be sure it is up to date and has general coverage. Such books are normally available at your library, and the librarian will be glad to help you locate one. For entry-level positions, questions of appropriate difficulty are chosen – neither highly advanced questions, nor those too simple. Such questions require careful thought but not advanced training.

If the position for which you are applying is technical or advanced, you will read more advanced, specialized material. If you are already familiar with the basic principles of your field, elementary textbooks would waste your time. Concentrate on advanced textbooks and technical periodicals. Think through the concepts and review difficult problems in your field.

These are all general sources. You can get more ideas on your own initiative, following these leads. For example, training manuals and publications of the government agency which employs workers in your field can be useful, particularly for technical and professional positions. A letter or visit to the government department involved may result in more specific study suggestions, and certainly will provide you with a more definite idea of the exact nature of the position you are seeking.

III. KINDS OF TESTS

Tests are used for purposes other than measuring knowledge and ability to perform specified duties. For some positions, it is equally important to test ability to make adjustments to new situations or to profit from training. In others, basic mental abilities not dependent on information are essential. Questions which test these things may not appear as pertinent to the duties of the position as those which test for knowledge and information. Yet they are often highly important parts of a fair examination. For very general questions, it is almost impossible to help you direct your study efforts. What we can do is to point out some of the more common of these general abilities needed in public service positions and describe some typical questions.

1) General information

Broad, general information has been found useful for predicting job success in some kinds of work. This is tested in a variety of ways, from vocabulary lists to questions about current events. Basic background in some field of work, such as sociology or economics, may be sampled in a group of questions. Often these are principles which have become familiar to most persons through exposure rather than through formal training. It is difficult to advise you how to study for these questions; being alert to the world around you is our best suggestion.

2) Verbal ability

An example of an ability needed in many positions is verbal or language ability. Verbal ability is, in brief, the ability to use and understand words. Vocabulary and grammar tests are typical measures of this ability. Reading comprehension or paragraph interpretation questions are common in many kinds of civil service tests. You are given a paragraph of written material and asked to find its central meaning.

3) Numerical ability

Number skills can be tested by the familiar arithmetic problem, by checking paired lists of numbers to see which are alike and which are different, or by interpreting charts and graphs. In the latter test, a graph may be printed in the test booklet which you are asked to use as the basis for answering questions.

4) Observation

A popular test for law-enforcement positions is the observation test. A picture is shown to you for several minutes, then taken away. Questions about the picture test your ability to observe both details and larger elements.

5) Following directions

In many positions in the public service, the employee must be able to carry out written instructions dependably and accurately. You may be given a chart with several columns, each column listing a variety of information. The questions require you to carry out directions involving the information given in the chart.

6) Skills and aptitudes

Performance tests effectively measure some manual skills and aptitudes. When the skill is one in which you are trained, such as typing or shorthand, you can practice. These tests are often very much like those given in business school or high school courses. For many of the other skills and aptitudes, however, no short-time preparation can be made. Skills and abilities natural to you or that you have developed throughout your lifetime are being tested.

Many of the general questions just described provide all the data needed to answer the questions and ask you to use your reasoning ability to find the answers. Your best preparation for these tests, as well as for tests of facts and ideas, is to be at your physical and mental best. You, no doubt, have your own methods of getting into an exam-taking mood and keeping "in shape." The next section lists some ideas on this subject.

IV. KINDS OF QUESTIONS

Only rarely is the "essay" question, which you answer in narrative form, used in civil service tests. Civil service tests are usually of the short-answer type. Full instructions for answering these questions will be given to you at the examination. But in case this is your first experience with short-answer questions and separate answer sheets, here is what you need to know:

1) Multiple-choice Questions

Most popular of the short-answer questions is the "multiple choice" or "best answer" question. It can be used, for example, to test for factual knowledge, ability to solve problems or judgment in meeting situations found at work.

A multiple-choice question is normally one of three types—

- It can begin with an incomplete statement followed by several possible endings. You are to find the one ending which *best* completes the statement, although some of the others may not be entirely wrong.
- It can also be a complete statement in the form of a question which is answered by choosing one of the statements listed.

- It can be in the form of a problem – again you select the best answer.

Here is an example of a multiple-choice question with a discussion which should give you some clues as to the method for choosing the right answer:

When an employee has a complaint about his assignment, the action which will *best* help him overcome his difficulty is to
- A. discuss his difficulty with his coworkers
- B. take the problem to the head of the organization
- C. take the problem to the person who gave him the assignment
- D. say nothing to anyone about his complaint

In answering this question, you should study each of the choices to find which is best. Consider choice "A" – Certainly an employee may discuss his complaint with fellow employees, but no change or improvement can result, and the complaint remains unresolved. Choice "B" is a poor choice since the head of the organization probably does not know what assignment you have been given, and taking your problem to him is known as "going over the head" of the supervisor. The supervisor, or person who made the assignment, is the person who can clarify it or correct any injustice. Choice "C" is, therefore, correct. To say nothing, as in choice "D," is unwise. Supervisors have and interest in knowing the problems employees are facing, and the employee is seeking a solution to his problem.

2) True/False Questions

The "true/false" or "right/wrong" form of question is sometimes used. Here a complete statement is given. Your job is to decide whether the statement is right or wrong.

SAMPLE: A roaming cell-phone call to a nearby city costs less than a non-roaming call to a distant city.

This statement is wrong, or false, since roaming calls are more expensive.

This is not a complete list of all possible question forms, although most of the others are variations of these common types. You will always get complete directions for answering questions. Be sure you understand *how* to mark your answers – ask questions until you do.

V. RECORDING YOUR ANSWERS

Computer terminals are used more and more today for many different kinds of exams.

For an examination with very few applicants, you may be told to record your answers in the test booklet itself. Separate answer sheets are much more common. If this separate answer sheet is to be scored by machine – and this is often the case – it is highly important that you mark your answers correctly in order to get credit.

An electronic scoring machine is often used in civil service offices because of the speed with which papers can be scored. Machine-scored answer sheets must be marked with a pencil, which will be given to you. This pencil has a high graphite content which responds to the electronic scoring machine. As a matter of fact, stray dots may register as answers, so do not let your pencil rest on the answer sheet while you are pondering the correct answer. Also, if your pencil lead breaks or is otherwise defective, ask for another.

Since the answer sheet will be dropped in a slot in the scoring machine, be careful not to bend the corners or get the paper crumpled.

The answer sheet normally has five vertical columns of numbers, with 30 numbers to a column. These numbers correspond to the question numbers in your test booklet. After each number, going across the page are four or five pairs of dotted lines. These short dotted lines have small letters or numbers above them. The first two pairs may also have a "T" or "F" above the letters. This indicates that the first two pairs only are to be used if the questions are of the true-false type. If the questions are multiple choice, disregard the "T" and "F" and pay attention only to the small letters or numbers.

Answer your questions in the manner of the sample that follows:

32. The largest city in the United States is
    A. Washington, D.C.
    B. New York City
    C. Chicago
    D. Detroit
    E. San Francisco

1) Choose the answer you think is best. (New York City is the largest, so "B" is correct.)
2) Find the row of dotted lines numbered the same as the question you are answering. (Find row number 32)
3) Find the pair of dotted lines corresponding to the answer. (Find the pair of lines under the mark "B.")
4) Make a solid black mark between the dotted lines.

VI. BEFORE THE TEST

Common sense will help you find procedures to follow to get ready for an examination. Too many of us, however, overlook these sensible measures. Indeed, nervousness and fatigue have been found to be the most serious reasons why applicants fail to do their best on civil service tests. Here is a list of reminders:

- Begin your preparation early – Don't wait until the last minute to go scurrying around for books and materials or to find out what the position is all about.
- Prepare continuously – An hour a night for a week is better than an all-night cram session. This has been definitely established. What is more, a night a week for a month will return better dividends than crowding your study into a shorter period of time.
- Locate the place of the exam – You have been sent a notice telling you when and where to report for the examination. If the location is in a different town or otherwise unfamiliar to you, it would be well to inquire the best route and learn something about the building.
- Relax the night before the test – Allow your mind to rest. Do not study at all that night. Plan some mild recreation or diversion; then go to bed early and get a good night's sleep.
- Get up early enough to make a leisurely trip to the place for the test – This way unforeseen events, traffic snarls, unfamiliar buildings, etc. will not upset you.
- Dress comfortably – A written test is not a fashion show. You will be known by number and not by name, so wear something comfortable.

- Leave excess paraphernalia at home – Shopping bags and odd bundles will get in your way. You need bring only the items mentioned in the official notice you received; usually everything you need is provided. Do not bring reference books to the exam. They will only confuse those last minutes and be taken away from you when in the test room.
- Arrive somewhat ahead of time – If because of transportation schedules you must get there very early, bring a newspaper or magazine to take your mind off yourself while waiting.
- Locate the examination room – When you have found the proper room, you will be directed to the seat or part of the room where you will sit. Sometimes you are given a sheet of instructions to read while you are waiting. Do not fill out any forms until you are told to do so; just read them and be prepared.
- Relax and prepare to listen to the instructions
- If you have any physical problem that may keep you from doing your best, be sure to tell the test administrator. If you are sick or in poor health, you really cannot do your best on the exam. You can come back and take the test some other time.

VII. AT THE TEST

The day of the test is here and you have the test booklet in your hand. The temptation to get going is very strong. Caution! There is more to success than knowing the right answers. You must know how to identify your papers and understand variations in the type of short-answer question used in this particular examination. Follow these suggestions for maximum results from your efforts:

1) Cooperate with the monitor

The test administrator has a duty to create a situation in which you can be as much at ease as possible. He will give instructions, tell you when to begin, check to see that you are marking your answer sheet correctly, and so on. He is not there to guard you, although he will see that your competitors do not take unfair advantage. He wants to help you do your best.

2) Listen to all instructions

Don't jump the gun! Wait until you understand all directions. In most civil service tests you get more time than you need to answer the questions. So don't be in a hurry. Read each word of instructions until you clearly understand the meaning. Study the examples, listen to all announcements and follow directions. Ask questions if you do not understand what to do.

3) Identify your papers

Civil service exams are usually identified by number only. You will be assigned a number; you must not put your name on your test papers. Be sure to copy your number correctly. Since more than one exam may be given, copy your exact examination title.

4) Plan your time

Unless you are told that a test is a "speed" or "rate of work" test, speed itself is usually not important. Time enough to answer all the questions will be provided, but this does not mean that you have all day. An overall time limit has been set. Divide the total time (in minutes) by the number of questions to determine the approximate time you have for each question.

5) Do not linger over difficult questions

If you come across a difficult question, mark it with a paper clip (useful to have along) and come back to it when you have been through the booklet. One caution if you do this – be sure to skip a number on your answer sheet as well. Check often to be sure that you have not lost your place and that you are marking in the row numbered the same as the question you are answering.

6) Read the questions

Be sure you know what the question asks! Many capable people are unsuccessful because they failed to *read* the questions correctly.

7) Answer all questions

Unless you have been instructed that a penalty will be deducted for incorrect answers, it is better to guess than to omit a question.

8) Speed tests

It is often better NOT to guess on speed tests. It has been found that on timed tests people are tempted to spend the last few seconds before time is called in marking answers at random – without even reading them – in the hope of picking up a few extra points. To discourage this practice, the instructions may warn you that your score will be "corrected" for guessing. That is, a penalty will be applied. The incorrect answers will be deducted from the correct ones, or some other penalty formula will be used.

9) Review your answers

If you finish before time is called, go back to the questions you guessed or omitted to give them further thought. Review other answers if you have time.

10) Return your test materials

If you are ready to leave before others have finished or time is called, take ALL your materials to the monitor and leave quietly. Never take any test material with you. The monitor can discover whose papers are not complete, and taking a test booklet may be grounds for disqualification.

VIII. EXAMINATION TECHNIQUES

1) Read the general instructions carefully. These are usually printed on the first page of the exam booklet. As a rule, these instructions refer to the timing of the examination; the fact that you should not start work until the signal and must stop work at a signal, etc. If there are any *special* instructions, such as a choice of questions to be answered, make sure that you note this instruction carefully.

2) When you are ready to start work on the examination, that is as soon as the signal has been given, read the instructions to each question booklet, underline any key words or phrases, such as *least, best, outline, describe* and the like. In this way you will tend to answer as requested rather than discover on reviewing your paper that you *listed without describing*, that you selected the *worst* choice rather than the *best* choice, etc.

3) If the examination is of the objective or multiple-choice type – that is, each question will also give a series of possible answers: A, B, C or D, and you are called upon to select the best answer and write the letter next to that answer on your answer paper – it is advisable to start answering each question in turn. There may be anywhere from 50 to 100 such questions in the three or four hours allotted and you can see how much time would be taken if you read through all the questions before beginning to answer any. Furthermore, if you come across a question or group of questions which you know would be difficult to answer, it would undoubtedly affect your handling of all the other questions.

4) If the examination is of the essay type and contains but a few questions, it is a moot point as to whether you should read all the questions before starting to answer any one. Of course, if you are given a choice – say five out of seven and the like – then it is essential to read all the questions so you can eliminate the two that are most difficult. If, however, you are asked to answer all the questions, there may be danger in trying to answer the easiest one first because you may find that you will spend too much time on it. The best technique is to answer the first question, then proceed to the second, etc.

5) Time your answers. Before the exam begins, write down the time it started, then add the time allowed for the examination and write down the time it must be completed, then divide the time available somewhat as follows:
    - If 3-1/2 hours are allowed, that would be 210 minutes. If you have 80 objective-type questions, that would be an average of 2-1/2 minutes per question. Allow yourself no more than 2 minutes per question, or a total of 160 minutes, which will permit about 50 minutes to review.
    - If for the time allotment of 210 minutes there are 7 essay questions to answer, that would average about 30 minutes a question. Give yourself only 25 minutes per question so that you have about 35 minutes to review.

6) The most important instruction is to *read each question* and make sure you know what is wanted. The second most important instruction is to *time yourself properly* so that you answer every question. The third most important instruction is to *answer every question*. Guess if you have to but include something for each question. Remember that you will receive no credit for a blank and will probably receive some credit if you write something in answer to an essay question. If you guess a letter – say "B" for a multiple-choice question – you may have guessed right. If you leave a blank as an answer to a multiple-choice question, the examiners may respect your feelings but it will not add a point to your score. Some exams may penalize you for wrong answers, so in such cases *only*, you may not want to guess unless you have some basis for your answer.

7) Suggestions
    a. Objective-type questions
        1. Examine the question booklet for proper sequence of pages and questions
        2. Read all instructions carefully
        3. Skip any question which seems too difficult; return to it after all other questions have been answered
        4. Apportion your time properly; do not spend too much time on any single question or group of questions

5. Note and underline key words – *all, most, fewest, least, best, worst, same, opposite*, etc.
6. Pay particular attention to negatives
7. Note unusual option, e.g., unduly long, short, complex, different or similar in content to the body of the question
8. Observe the use of "hedging" words – *probably, may, most likely*, etc.
9. Make sure that your answer is put next to the same number as the question
10. Do not second-guess unless you have good reason to believe the second answer is definitely more correct
11. Cross out original answer if you decide another answer is more accurate; do not erase until you are ready to hand your paper in
12. Answer all questions; guess unless instructed otherwise
13. Leave time for review

   b. Essay questions
   1. Read each question carefully
   2. Determine exactly what is wanted. Underline key words or phrases.
   3. Decide on outline or paragraph answer
   4. Include many different points and elements unless asked to develop any one or two points or elements
   5. Show impartiality by giving pros and cons unless directed to select one side only
   6. Make and write down any assumptions you find necessary to answer the questions
   7. Watch your English, grammar, punctuation and choice of words
   8. Time your answers; don't crowd material

8) Answering the essay question

Most essay questions can be answered by framing the specific response around several key words or ideas. Here are a few such key words or ideas:

M's: manpower, materials, methods, money, management
P's: purpose, program, policy, plan, procedure, practice, problems, pitfalls, personnel, public relations

   a. Six basic steps in handling problems:
   1. Preliminary plan and background development
   2. Collect information, data and facts
   3. Analyze and interpret information, data and facts
   4. Analyze and develop solutions as well as make recommendations
   5. Prepare report and sell recommendations
   6. Install recommendations and follow up effectiveness

   b. Pitfalls to avoid
   1. *Taking things for granted* – A statement of the situation does not necessarily imply that each of the elements is necessarily true; for example, a complaint may be invalid and biased so that all that can be taken for granted is that a complaint has been registered

2. *Considering only one side of a situation* – Wherever possible, indicate several alternatives and then point out the reasons you selected the best one
3. *Failing to indicate follow up* – Whenever your answer indicates action on your part, make certain that you will take proper follow-up action to see how successful your recommendations, procedures or actions turn out to be
4. *Taking too long in answering any single question* – Remember to time your answers properly

IX. AFTER THE TEST

Scoring procedures differ in detail among civil service jurisdictions although the general principles are the same. Whether the papers are hand-scored or graded by machine we have described, they are nearly always graded by number. That is, the person who marks the paper knows only the number – never the name – of the applicant. Not until all the papers have been graded will they be matched with names. If other tests, such as training and experience or oral interview ratings have been given, scores will be combined. Different parts of the examination usually have different weights. For example, the written test might count 60 percent of the final grade, and a rating of training and experience 40 percent. In many jurisdictions, veterans will have a certain number of points added to their grades.

After the final grade has been determined, the names are placed in grade order and an eligible list is established. There are various methods for resolving ties between those who get the same final grade – probably the most common is to place first the name of the person whose application was received first. Job offers are made from the eligible list in the order the names appear on it. You will be notified of your grade and your rank as soon as all these computations have been made. This will be done as rapidly as possible.

People who are found to meet the requirements in the announcement are called "eligibles." Their names are put on a list of eligible candidates. An eligible's chances of getting a job depend on how high he stands on this list and how fast agencies are filling jobs from the list.

When a job is to be filled from a list of eligibles, the agency asks for the names of people on the list of eligibles for that job. When the civil service commission receives this request, it sends to the agency the names of the three people highest on this list. Or, if the job to be filled has specialized requirements, the office sends the agency the names of the top three persons who meet these requirements from the general list.

The appointing officer makes a choice from among the three people whose names were sent to him. If the selected person accepts the appointment, the names of the others are put back on the list to be considered for future openings.

That is the rule in hiring from all kinds of eligible lists, whether they are for typist, carpenter, chemist, or something else. For every vacancy, the appointing officer has his choice of any one of the top three eligibles on the list. This explains why the person whose name is on top of the list sometimes does not get an appointment when some of the persons lower on the list do. If the appointing officer chooses the second or third eligible, the No. 1 eligible does not get a job at once, but stays on the list until he is appointed or the list is terminated.

X. HOW TO PASS THE INTERVIEW TEST

The examination for which you applied requires an oral interview test. You have already taken the written test and you are now being called for the interview test – the final part of the formal examination.

You may think that it is not possible to prepare for an interview test and that there are no procedures to follow during an interview. Our purpose is to point out some things you can do in advance that will help you and some good rules to follow and pitfalls to avoid while you are being interviewed.

What is an interview supposed to test?

The written examination is designed to test the technical knowledge and competence of the candidate; the oral is designed to evaluate intangible qualities, not readily measured otherwise, and to establish a list showing the relative fitness of each candidate – as measured against his competitors – for the position sought. Scoring is not on the basis of "right" and "wrong," but on a sliding scale of values ranging from "not passable" to "outstanding." As a matter of fact, it is possible to achieve a relatively low score without a single "incorrect" answer because of evident weakness in the qualities being measured.

Occasionally, an examination may consist entirely of an oral test – either an individual or a group oral. In such cases, information is sought concerning the technical knowledges and abilities of the candidate, since there has been no written examination for this purpose. More commonly, however, an oral test is used to supplement a written examination.

Who conducts interviews?

The composition of oral boards varies among different jurisdictions. In nearly all, a representative of the personnel department serves as chairman. One of the members of the board may be a representative of the department in which the candidate would work. In some cases, "outside experts" are used, and, frequently, a businessman or some other representative of the general public is asked to serve. Labor and management or other special groups may be represented. The aim is to secure the services of experts in the appropriate field.

However the board is composed, it is a good idea (and not at all improper or unethical) to ascertain in advance of the interview who the members are and what groups they represent. When you are introduced to them, you will have some idea of their backgrounds and interests, and at least you will not stutter and stammer over their names.

What should be done before the interview?

While knowledge about the board members is useful and takes some of the surprise element out of the interview, there is other preparation which is more substantive. It *is* possible to prepare for an oral interview – in several ways:

1) Keep a copy of your application and review it carefully before the interview

This may be the only document before the oral board, and the starting point of the interview. Know what education and experience you have listed there, and the sequence and dates of all of it. Sometimes the board will ask you to review the highlights of your experience for them; you should not have to hem and haw doing it.

2) Study the class specification and the examination announcement

Usually, the oral board has one or both of these to guide them. The qualities, characteristics or knowledges required by the position sought are stated in these documents. They offer valuable clues as to the nature of the oral interview. For example, if the job involves supervisory responsibilities, the announcement will usually indicate that knowledge of modern supervisory methods and the qualifications of the candidate as a supervisor will be tested. If so, you can expect such questions, frequently in the form of a hypothetical situation which you are expected to solve. NEVER go into an oral without knowledge of the duties and responsibilities of the job you seek.

3) Think through each qualification required

Try to visualize the kind of questions you would ask if you were a board member. How well could you answer them? Try especially to appraise your own knowledge and background in each area, *measured against the job sought*, and identify any areas in which you are weak. Be critical and realistic – do not flatter yourself.

4) Do some general reading in areas in which you feel you may be weak

For example, if the job involves supervision and your past experience has NOT, some general reading in supervisory methods and practices, particularly in the field of human relations, might be useful. Do NOT study agency procedures or detailed manuals. The oral board will be testing your understanding and capacity, not your memory.

5) Get a good night's sleep and watch your general health and mental attitude

You will want a clear head at the interview. Take care of a cold or any other minor ailment, and of course, no hangovers.

What should be done on the day of the interview?

Now comes the day of the interview itself. Give yourself plenty of time to get there. Plan to arrive somewhat ahead of the scheduled time, particularly if your appointment is in the fore part of the day. If a previous candidate fails to appear, the board might be ready for you a bit early. By early afternoon an oral board is almost invariably behind schedule if there are many candidates, and you may have to wait. Take along a book or magazine to read, or your application to review, but leave any extraneous material in the waiting room when you go in for your interview. In any event, relax and compose yourself.

The matter of dress is important. The board is forming impressions about you – from your experience, your manners, your attitude, and your appearance. Give your personal appearance careful attention. Dress your best, but not your flashiest. Choose conservative, appropriate clothing, and be sure it is immaculate. This is a business interview, and your appearance should indicate that you regard it as such. Besides, being well groomed and properly dressed will help boost your confidence.

Sooner or later, someone will call your name and escort you into the interview room. *This is it.* From here on you are on your own. It is too late for any more preparation. But remember, you asked for this opportunity to prove your fitness, and you are here because your request was granted.

What happens when you go in?

The usual sequence of events will be as follows: The clerk (who is often the board stenographer) will introduce you to the chairman of the oral board, who will introduce you to the other members of the board. Acknowledge the introductions before you sit down. Do not be surprised if you find a microphone facing you or a stenotypist sitting by. Oral interviews are usually recorded in the event of an appeal or other review.

Usually the chairman of the board will open the interview by reviewing the highlights of your education and work experience from your application – primarily for the benefit of the other members of the board, as well as to get the material into the record. Do not interrupt or comment unless there is an error or significant misinterpretation; if that is the case, do not hesitate. But do not quibble about insignificant matters. Also, he will usually ask you some question about your education, experience or your present job – partly to get you to start talking and to establish the interviewing "rapport." He may start the actual questioning, or turn it over to one of the other members. Frequently, each member undertakes the questioning on a particular area, one in which he is perhaps most competent, so you can expect each member to participate in the examination. Because time is limited, you may also expect some rather abrupt switches in the direction the questioning takes, so do not be upset by it. Normally, a board member will not pursue a single line of questioning unless he discovers a particular strength or weakness.

After each member has participated, the chairman will usually ask whether any member has any further questions, then will ask you if you have anything you wish to add. Unless you are expecting this question, it may floor you. Worse, it may start you off on an extended, extemporaneous speech. The board is not usually seeking more information. The question is principally to offer you a last opportunity to present further qualifications or to indicate that you have nothing to add. So, if you feel that a significant qualification or characteristic has been overlooked, it is proper to point it out in a sentence or so. Do not compliment the board on the thoroughness of their examination – they have been sketchy, and you know it. If you wish, merely say, "No thank you, I have nothing further to add." This is a point where you can "talk yourself out" of a good impression or fail to present an important bit of information. Remember, *you close the interview yourself*.

The chairman will then say, "That is all, Mr. _____, thank you." Do not be startled; the interview is over, and quicker than you think. Thank him, gather your belongings and take your leave. Save your sigh of relief for the other side of the door.

How to put your best foot forward

Throughout this entire process, you may feel that the board individually and collectively is trying to pierce your defenses, seek out your hidden weaknesses and embarrass and confuse you. Actually, this is not true. They are obliged to make an appraisal of your qualifications for the job you are seeking, and they want to see you in your best light. Remember, they must interview all candidates and a non-cooperative candidate may become a failure in spite of their best efforts to bring out his qualifications. Here are 15 suggestions that will help you:

1) Be natural – Keep your attitude confident, not cocky

If you are not confident that you can do the job, do not expect the board to be. Do not apologize for your weaknesses, try to bring out your strong points. The board is interested in a positive, not negative, presentation. Cockiness will antagonize any board member and make him wonder if you are covering up a weakness by a false show of strength.

2) Get comfortable, but don't lounge or sprawl

Sit erectly but not stiffly. A careless posture may lead the board to conclude that you are careless in other things, or at least that you are not impressed by the importance of the occasion. Either conclusion is natural, even if incorrect. Do not fuss with your clothing, a pencil or an ashtray. Your hands may occasionally be useful to emphasize a point; do not let them become a point of distraction.

3) Do not wisecrack or make small talk

This is a serious situation, and your attitude should show that you consider it as such. Further, the time of the board is limited – they do not want to waste it, and neither should you.

4) Do not exaggerate your experience or abilities

In the first place, from information in the application or other interviews and sources, the board may know more about you than you think. Secondly, you probably will not get away with it. An experienced board is rather adept at spotting such a situation, so do not take the chance.

5) If you know a board member, do not make a point of it, yet do not hide it

Certainly you are not fooling him, and probably not the other members of the board. Do not try to take advantage of your acquaintanceship – it will probably do you little good.

6) Do not dominate the interview

Let the board do that. They will give you the clues – do not assume that you have to do all the talking. Realize that the board has a number of questions to ask you, and do not try to take up all the interview time by showing off your extensive knowledge of the answer to the first one.

7) Be attentive

You only have 20 minutes or so, and you should keep your attention at its sharpest throughout. When a member is addressing a problem or question to you, give him your undivided attention. Address your reply principally to him, but do not exclude the other board members.

8) Do not interrupt

A board member may be stating a problem for you to analyze. He will ask you a question when the time comes. Let him state the problem, and wait for the question.

9) Make sure you understand the question

Do not try to answer until you are sure what the question is. If it is not clear, restate it in your own words or ask the board member to clarify it for you. However, do not haggle about minor elements.

10) Reply promptly but not hastily

A common entry on oral board rating sheets is "candidate responded readily," or "candidate hesitated in replies." Respond as promptly and quickly as you can, but do not jump to a hasty, ill-considered answer.

11) Do not be peremptory in your answers

A brief answer is proper – but do not fire your answer back. That is a losing game from your point of view. The board member can probably ask questions much faster than you can answer them.

12) Do not try to create the answer you think the board member wants

He is interested in what kind of mind you have and how it works – not in playing games. Furthermore, he can usually spot this practice and will actually grade you down on it.

13) Do not switch sides in your reply merely to agree with a board member

Frequently, a member will take a contrary position merely to draw you out and to see if you are willing and able to defend your point of view. Do not start a debate, yet do not surrender a good position. If a position is worth taking, it is worth defending.

14) Do not be afraid to admit an error in judgment if you are shown to be wrong

The board knows that you are forced to reply without any opportunity for careful consideration. Your answer may be demonstrably wrong. If so, admit it and get on with the interview.

15) Do not dwell at length on your present job

The opening question may relate to your present assignment. Answer the question but do not go into an extended discussion. You are being examined for a *new* job, not your present one. As a matter of fact, try to phrase ALL your answers in terms of the job for which you are being examined.

Basis of Rating

Probably you will forget most of these "do's" and "don'ts" when you walk into the oral interview room. Even remembering them all will not ensure you a passing grade. Perhaps you did not have the qualifications in the first place. But remembering them will help you to put your best foot forward, without treading on the toes of the board members.

Rumor and popular opinion to the contrary notwithstanding, an oral board wants you to make the best appearance possible. They know you are under pressure – but they also want to see how you respond to it as a guide to what your reaction would be under the pressures of the job you seek. They will be influenced by the degree of poise you display, the personal traits you show and the manner in which you respond.

ABOUT THIS BOOK

This book contains tests divided into Examination Sections. Go through each test, answering every question in the margin. We have also attached a sample answer sheet at the back of the book that can be removed and used. At the end of each test look at the answer key and check your answers. On the ones you got wrong, look at the right answer choice and learn. Do not fill in the answers first. Do not memorize the questions and answers, but understand the answer and principles involved. On your test, the questions will likely be different from the samples. Questions are changed and new ones added. If you understand these past questions you should have success with any changes that arise. Tests may consist of several types of questions. We have additional books on each subject should more study be advisable or necessary for you. Finally, the more you study, the better prepared you will be. This book is intended to be the last thing you study before you walk into the examination room. Prior study of relevant texts is also recommended. NLC publishes some of these in our Fundamental Series. Knowledge and good sense are important factors in passing your exam. Good luck also helps. So now study this Passbook, absorb the material contained within and take that knowledge into the examination. Then do your best to pass that exam.

EXAMINATION SECTION

EXAMINATION SECTION
TEST 1

DIRECTIONS: Each question or incomplete statement is followed by several suggested answers or completions. Select the one that BEST answers the question or completes the statement. *PRINT THE LETTER OF THE CORRECT ANSWER IN THE SPACE AT THE RIGHT.*

1. In the preparation of a balance sheet, failure to consider the inventory of office supplies will result in _____ assets and _____.

    A. overstating; overstating liabilities
    B. understating; overstating capital
    C. understating; understating capital
    D. overstating; understating liabilities

2. The annual federal unemployment tax is paid by the

    A. employer *only*
    B. employee *only*
    C. employer and the employee equally
    D. employee, up to a maximum of 30 cents per week, and the balance is paid by the employer

3. Which are NORMALLY considered as current assets?

    A. Bank overdrafts B. Prepaid expenses
    C. Accrued expenses D. Payroll taxes

4. What type of ledger account is a summary of a number of accounts in another ledger? The _____ account.

    A. controlling B. subsidiary
    C. asset D. proprietorship

5. The PRIMARY purpose of a petty cash fund is to

    A. provide a fund for paying all miscellaneous expenses
    B. take the place of the cash account
    C. provide a common drawing fund for the owners of the business
    D. avoid entering a number of small amounts in the Cash Payments Journal

6. In the absence of a written agreement, profits in a partnership would be divided

    A. in proportion to the investment of the partners
    B. on an equitable basis depending on the time and effort spent by the partners
    C. equally
    D. on a ratio of investment basis, giving the senior partner preference

7. Which account represents a subtraction or decrease to an income account?

    A. Purchase Returns & Allowances
    B. Sales Returns & Allowances
    C. Freight In
    D. Prepaid Rent

8. If the Interest Expense account showed a debit balance of $210 as of December 31, and $40 of this amount was prepaid on Notes Payable, which statement is CORRECT as of December 31?

   A. Prepaid Interest of $170 should be shown as a deferred expense in the balance sheet.
   B. Interest Expense should be shown in the Income Statement as $210.
   C. Prepaid Interest of $40 should be listed as a deferred credit to income in the balance sheet.
   D. Interest Expense should be shown in the Income Statement as $170.

9. When prices are rising, which inventory-valuation method results in the LOWEST inventory value?

   A. FIFO
   B. LIFO
   C. Average cost
   D. Declining balance

10. Which of the following is a CORRECT procedure in preparing a bank reconciliation?

    A. Deposits in transit should be added to the cash balance on the books, and outstanding checks should be deducted from the cash balance on the bank statement.
    B. The cash balance on the bank statement and the cash balance on the books should be equal if there are deposits in transit and outstanding checks.
    C. Outstanding checks should be deducted from the cash balance on the books.
    D. Any service charge should be deducted from the check stub balance.

11. Which ratio indicates that there may NOT be enough on hand to meet current obligations?

    A. $\dfrac{\text{fixed assets}}{\text{fixed liabilities}} = \dfrac{2}{3}$
    B. $\dfrac{\text{total assets}}{\text{total obligations}} = \dfrac{3}{5}$
    C. $\dfrac{\text{current assets}}{\text{current liabilities}} = \dfrac{1}{3}$
    D. $\dfrac{\text{current assets}}{\text{fixed liabilities}} = \dfrac{1}{2}$

12. Which asset is NOT subject to depreciation?

    A. Factory equipment
    B. Land
    C. Buildings
    D. Machinery

13. Which form is prepared to verify that the total of the account balances in the Customers Ledger agrees with the balance in the controlling account in the General Ledger?

    A. Worksheet
    B. Schedule of accounts payable
    C. Schedule of accounts receivable
    D. Trial balance

14. If the merchandise inventory on hand at the end of the year was overstated, what will be the result of this error?

    A. *Understatement* of income for the year
    B. *Overstatement* of income for the year
    C. *Understatement* of assets at the end of the year
    D. No effect on income or assets

15. Working capital is found by subtracting the total current liabilities from the total

    A. fixed liabilities
    B. fixed assets
    C. current income
    D. current assets

16. Which is the CORRECT procedure for calculating the rate of merchandise turnover?

    A. Gross Sales divided by Net Sales
    B. Cost of Sales divided by Average Inventory
    C. Net Purchases divided by Average Inventory
    D. Gross Purchases divided by Net Purchases

17. The books of the Atlas Cement Corporation show a net profit of $142,000. To close the Profit and Loss account of the corporation at the end of the year, the account CREDITED should be

    A. Earned Surplus
    B. Capital Stock
    C. C. Atlas, Capital
    D. C. Atlas, Personal

18. The bank statement at the end of the month indicated a bank charge for printing a new checkbook.
    How is this information recorded?
    Debit

    A. Cash and credit Office Supplies
    B. Office Supplies and credit the Bank Charges
    C. the Bank Charges and credit Office Supplies
    D. Miscellaneous Expense and credit Cash

19. The Allowance for Doubtful Accounts appears on the balance sheet as a deduction from

    A. Accounts Receivable
    B. Notes Receivable
    C. Accounts Payable
    D. Notes Payable

20. The Tucker Equipment Corporation had a $45,000 profit for the year ended December 31.
    Which would be the PROPER entry to close the Income and Expense account at the end of the year?
    Debit Income and Expense Summary; credit

    A. Tucker, Capital
    B. Tucker, Drawing
    C. Retained Earnings
    D. Capital Stock

21. A failure to record a purchases invoice would be discovered when the

    A. monthly statement of account is sent to the customer
    B. check is received from the customer
    C. check is sent to the creditor
    D. statement of account is received from the creditor

22. Which General Ledger account would appear in a post-closing trial balance?

    A. Notes Receivable
    B. Bad Debts Expense
    C. Sales Discount
    D. Fee Income

23. Which deduction is affected by the number of exemptions claimed?

    A. State Disability
    B. State income tax
    C. FICA tax
    D. Workers' Compensation

24. The face value of a 60-day, 12% promissory note is $900.
    The maturity value of this note will be

    A. $909   B. $900   C. $918   D. $1,008

25. An invoice dated March 10, terms 2/10, n/30, should be paid no later than

    A. March 20   B. March 31   C. April 9   D. April 10

KEY (CORRECT ANSWERS)

1. C   11. C
2. A   12. B
3. B   13. C
4. A   14. B
5. D   15. D

6. C   16. B
7. B   17. A
8. D   18. D
9. B   19. A
10. D   20. C

21. D
22. A
23. B
24. C
25. C

TEST 2

DIRECTIONS: Each question or incomplete statement is followed by several suggested answers or completions. Select the one that BEST answers the question or completes the statement. *PRINT THE LETTER OF THE CORRECT ANSWER IN THE SPACE AT THE RIGHT.*

1. Which is NOT an essential element of a computer system? 1.____

   A. Input
   B. Central processing unit
   C. Verifier
   D. Output

2. The general ledger account that would NOT appear in a post-closing trial balance would be 2.____

   A. Cash
   B. Accounts Payable
   C. Furniture and Fixtures
   D. Sales Income

3. Ralph Hanley, age 45, supports his wife and three children. Mr. Hanley is the only member of the family required to file an income tax return. What is the MAXIMUM number of exemptions he can claim? 3.____

   A. One   B. Five   C. Three   D. Four

4. The cost of a fixed asset minus the allowance for depreciation (accumulated depreciation) is the _____ value. 4.____

   A. market   B. cost   C. liquidation   D. book

5. The form used by a bookkeeper in summarizing adjustments and information which will be used in preparing statements is called a 5.____

   A. journal
   B. balance sheet
   C. ledger
   D. worksheet

6. When a large number of transactions of a particular kind are to be entered in bookkeeping records, it is USUALLY advisable to use 6.____

   A. cash records
   B. controlling accounts
   C. special journals
   D. special ledgers

7. The petty cash book shows a petty cash balance of $9.80 on May 31. The petty cash box contains only $9.10. What account will be debited to record the $.70 difference? 7.____

   A. Cash
   B. Petty Cash
   C. Cash Short and Over
   D. Petty Cash Expense

8. The ONLY difference between the books of a partnership and those of a sole proprietorship appears in the _____ accounts. 8.____

   A. proprietorship
   B. liability
   C. asset
   D. expense

9. The earnings of a corporation are FIRST recorded as a credit to an account called 9.____

   A. Dividends Payable
   B. Capital Stock Authorized
   C. Retained Earnings
   D. Profit and Loss Summary

10. A firm purchased a new delivery truck for $2,900 and sold it four years later for $500. The Allowance for Depreciation of Delivery Equipment account was credited for $580 at the end of each of the four years.
    When the machine was sold, there was a

    A. loss of $80
    B. loss of $1,820
    C. loss of $2,400
    D. gain of $80

11. FICA taxes are paid by

    A. employees *only*
    B. employers *only*
    C. both employees and employers
    D. neither employees nor employers

12. Which phase of the data processing cycle is the SAME as calculating net pay in a manual system?

    A. Input
    B. Processing
    C. Storing
    D. Output

13. Which error will cause the trial balance to be out of balance?

    A. A sales invoice for $60 was entered in the Sales Journal for $600.
    B. A credit to office furniture in the journal was posted as a credit to office machines in the ledger.
    C. A debit to advertising expense in the journal was posted as a debit to miscellaneous expense in the ledger.
    D. A debit to office equipment in the journal was posted as a credit to office equipment in the ledger.

14. The collection of a bad debt previously written off will result in a(n)

    A. *decrease* in assets
    B. *decrease* in capital
    C. *increase* in assets
    D. *increase* in liabilities

15. Which account does NOT belong in the group?

    A. Notes Receivable
    B. Building
    C. Office Equipment
    D. Delivery Truck

16. The adjusting entry to record the estimated bad debts is debit _____ and credit _____.

    A. Allowance for Bad Debts; Bad Debts Expense
    B. Bad Debts Expense; Allowance for Bad Debts
    C. Allowance for Bad Debts; Accounts Receivable
    D. Bad Debts Expense; Accounts Receivable

17. At the end of the year, which account should be closed into the income and expense summary?

    A. Freight In
    B. Allowance for Doubtful Accounts
    C. Notes Receivable
    D. Petty Cash

18. Which form is prepared to aid in verifying that the customer's account balances in the customer's ledger agree with the balance in the Accounts Receivable account in the general ledger?

    A. Worksheet
    B. Schedule of Accounts Payable
    C. Schedule of Accounts Receivable
    D. Trial Balance

19. In the preparation of an income statement, failure to consider accrued wages will result in

    A. *overstating* operating expense and understating net profit
    B. *overstating* net profit *only*
    C. *understating* operating expense and overstating net profit
    D. *understating* operating expense *only*

20. The CORRECT formula for determining the rate of merchandise turnover is

    A. cost of goods sold divided by average inventory
    B. net sales divided by net purchases
    C. gross sales divided by ending inventory
    D. average inventory divided by cost of goods sold

21. A legal characteristic of a corporation is _____ liability.

    A. contingent   B. limited
    C. unlimited   D. deferred

22. A customer's check you had deposited is returned to you by the bank labeled *Dishonored*.
    What entries would be made as a result of this action? Debit _____ and credit _____.

    A. cash; customer's account
    B. miscellaneous expense; cash
    C. customer's account; capital
    D. customer's account; cash

23. The TOTAL capital of a corporation may be found by adding

    A. assets and liabilities
    B. assets and capital stock
    C. liabilities and capital stock
    D. earned surplus and capital stock

24. The source of an entry made in the Petty Cash book is the

    A. general ledger   B. voucher
    C. register   D. general journal

25. Which account is debited to record interest earned but not yet due?

    A. Deferred Interest
    B. Interest Receivable
    C. Interest Income
    D. Income and Expense Summary

KEY (CORRECT ANSWERS)

1. C
2. D
3. B
4. D
5. D

6. C
7. C
8. A
9. C
10. A

11. C
12. B
13. D
14. C
15. A

16. B
17. A
18. C
19. C
20. A

21. B
22. D
23. D
24. B
25. B

TEST 3

DIRECTIONS: Each question or incomplete statement is followed by several suggested answers or completions. Select the one that BEST answers the question or completes the statement. *PRINT THE LETTER OF THE CORRECT ANSWER IN THE SPACE AT THE RIGHT.*

1. Which reason should NOT generally be used by an employer when making a hiring decision?
An applicant('s)

   A. resume reveals a lack of job-related skills
   B. attendance record on a previous job is poor
   C. has improperly prepared the job application
   D. is married

   1.____

2. Graves, Owens, and Smith formed a partnership and invested $15,000 each.
If the firm made a profit of $18,000 last year and profits and losses were shared equally, what was Owens' share of the net profit?

   A. $1,000   B. $5,000   C. $6,000   D. $9,000

   2.____

3. The bank statement balance of the Bedford Co. on May 31 was $3,263.28. The checkbook balance was $3,119.06. A reconciliation showed that the outstanding checks totaled $147.22 and that there was a bank service charge of $3.00. The CORRECT checkbook balance should be

   A. $3,260.28   B. $3,122.06   C. $3,116.06   D. $3,266.28

   3.____

4. Which account is shown in a post-closing trial balance?

   A. Prepaid Insurance   B. Fees Income
   C. Purchases   D. Freight In

   4.____

5. A check endorsed *For deposit only (signed) Samuel Jones* is an example of a _____ endorsement.

   A. full   B. blank   C. complete   D. restrictive

   5.____

6. The selling price of a share of stock as published in a daily newspaper is called the _____ value.

   A. book   B. face   C. par   D. market

   6.____

7. Which is obtained by dividing the cost of goods sold by the average inventory?

   A. Current ratio
   B. Merchandise inventory turnover
   C. Average rate of mark-up
   D. Acid-test ratio

   7.____

8. A Suzuki truck costing $39,000 is expected to have a useful life of six years and a salvage value of $3,000.
If $6,000 is debited to the depreciation expense account each year for six years, what method of depreciation is used?

   A. Units of production   B. Straight line
   C. Declining balance   D. Sum of the years digits

   8.____

9. Which form is prepared to aid in verifying that the customer's account balances in the customer's ledger agree with the balance in the Accounts Receivable account in the General Ledger?

    A. Worksheet
    B. Schedule of Accounts Payable
    C. Schedule of Accounts Receivable
    D. Trial Balance

10. In the preparation of a balance sheet, failure to consider commissions owed to salespersons will result in _____ liabilities and _____ capital.

    A. understating; overstating
    B. understating; understating
    C. overstating; overstating
    D. overstating; understating

11. A financial statement generated by a computer is an example of a(n)

    A. audit trail
    B. output
    C. input
    D. program

12. Merchandise was sold for $150 cash plus a 3% sales tax. The CORRECT credit(s) should be

    A. Sales Income $150, Sales Taxes Payable $4.50
    B. Sales Income $154.50
    C. Merchandise $150, Sales Taxes Payable $4.50
    D. Sales Income $150

13. The bookkeeper should prepare a bank reconciliation MAINLY to determine

    A. which checks are outstanding
    B. whether the checkbook balance and the bank statement balance are in agreement
    C. the total amount of checks written during the month
    D. the total amount of cash deposited during the month

14. Which is the CORRECT procedure for calculating the rate of merchandise turnover?

    A. Gross Sales divided by Net Sales
    B. Cost of Goods Sold divided by Average Inventory
    C. Net Purchases divided by Average Inventory
    D. Gross Purchases divided by Net Purchases

15. Which previous job should be listed FIRST on a job application form? The

    A. least recent job
    B. most recent job
    C. job you liked best
    D. job which paid the most

16. Failure to record cash sales will result in

    A. *overstatement* of profit
    B. *understatement* of profit
    C. *understatement* of liabilities
    D. *overstatement* of capital

17. When a fixed asset is repaired, the cost of the repairs should be _____ account.   17.____

    A. *debited* to the asset
    B. *debited* to the expense
    C. *credited* to the proprietor's capital
    D. *credited* to the asset

18. The form used by a bookkeeper to summarize information which will be used in preparing financial statements is called a   18.____

    A. journal   B. balance sheet
    C. ledger   D. worksheet

19. Which type of ledger account is a summary of a number of accounts in another ledger? _____ account.   19.____

    A. Controlling   B. Subsidiary
    C. Asset   D. Proprietorship

20. What is the summary entry on the Purchases Journal?
    Debit _____ and credit _____.   20.____

    A. Accounts Payable; Merchandise Purchases
    B. Accounts Receivable; Merchandise Purchases
    C. Merchandise Purchases; Accounts Receivable
    D. Merchandise Purchases; Accounts Payable

21. The source document for entries made in the Sales Journal is a(n)   21.____

    A. credit memo   B. statement of accounts
    C. invoice   D. bill of lading

22. A Trial Balance which is in balance would NOT reveal the   22.____

    A. omission of the credit part of an entry
    B. posting of the same debit twice
    C. omission of an entire transaction
    D. omission of an account with a balance

23. A financial statement prepared by a computerized accounting system is an example of   23.____

    A. input   B. output
    C. flowcharting   D. programming

24. The form which the payroll clerk gives to each employee to show gross earnings and taxes withheld for the year is a   24.____

    A. W-2   B. W-3   C. W-4   D. 1040

25. Who would be the LEAST appropriate reference on an application for a job?
    A   25.____

    A. relative
    B. guidance counselor
    C. former employer
    D. prominent member of the community

KEY (CORRECT ANSWERS)

1.	D	11.	B
2.	C	12.	A
3.	C	13.	B
4.	A	14.	B
5.	D	15.	B
6.	D	16.	B
7.	B	17.	B
8.	B	18.	D
9.	C	19.	A
10.	A	20.	D

21. C
22. C
23. B
24. A
25. A

EXAMINATION SECTION

TEST 1

DIRECTIONS: Each question or incomplete statement is followed by several suggested answers or completions. Select the one that BEST answers the question or completes the statement. *PRINT THE LETTER OF THE CORRECT ANSWER IN THE SPACE AT THE RIGHT.*

Questions 1-25.

DIRECTIONS: Below you will find the Cash Receipts Journal of John Walker, a merchant. Under the heading of each money column of the Journals, there is a letter of the alphabet. Following the Journals there is a series of transactions. You are to determine the entry for each transaction and then show in the space at the right the columns to be used.
 For example: If a certain transaction entered in the Cash Receipts Journal results in an entry of $100 in the General Ledger Column and $100 in the Net Cash Column, in the appropriate space at the right you should write: A,E. If the record of the transaction requires the use of more than two columns, your answer should contain more than two letters.
 Do not put the amounts in your answer space. The letters of the columns in the Cash Journals to be used are sufficient.
 If a transaction requires no entry in the Cash Journals, write "None" in the appropriate space at the right, even though a record would be made in some other journal.

CASH RECEIPTS JOURNAL

Date	Account Credited	Explanation	F	General Ledger	Accts. Rec.	Cash Sales	Disc. on Sales	Net Cash
				A	B	C	D	E

CASH PAYMENTS JOURNAL

Date	Acct. Debited	Explanation	F	General Ledger	Accts. Pay.	Soc. Sec. Taxes Pay.	With. Taxes Pay.	Disc. on Purch.	Net Cash
				F	G	H	I	J	K

1. Cash Sales amounted to $280.   1._____

2. Paid employees' salaries for the week. The check amounted to $346 after deducting $4.00 for Social Security Taxes and $30 for Income Taxes withheld.   2._____

3. A check received in the mail from R. Walters was in payment of a bill of $150, terms 2/10, n/30. The customer had taken the discount.   3._____

2 (#1)

4. The proprietor, Mr. Walker, took merchandise valued at $30 from the stockroom for his personal use.   4.____

5. Prepaid $15 freight on shipment of goods to H. Lane, a customer, and charged his account.   5.____

6. Sent a check for $250 to P. Packer to apply on account.   6.____

7. Drew a check for $75 to start a Petty Cash fund.   7.____

8. H. Wall sent us a check for $700 in payment of his 60-day note for $700. The note was interest bearing (6%), but he failed to pay us the interest. We deposited the $700 check and wrote to him requesting an additional check.   8.____

9. Paid rent for month $180.   9.____

10. Received a check for $70 from K. London to apply on account.   10.____

11. H. Wall sent us a check for the interest due on note (see Item 8).   11.____

12. Paid our 30-day note for $460 due today which we had given to G. Thompson.   12.____

13. Accepted a trade acceptance drawn by R. Sparks on us for invoice of $722.   13.____

14. Borrowed at our bank on our $1,500 note. Net proceeds, $1,485. (The bookkeeper used only one journal to make a complete and correct entry. You are to do likewise.)   14.____

15. Received a check for $60 from W. Saks, a creditor, refunding our overpayment to him on our account.   15.____

16. A check from H. Low, which was deposited by us last month, was returned to us marked "insufficient funds." The check amounted to $55 and had been sent to us to settle his account.   16.____

17. Drew a sight draft on R. Coe for overdue account of $120. Left draft at bank for collection.   17.____

18. Paid $26 freight on goods purchased from W. Lincoln of Chicago, terms f.o.b. Chicago.   18.____

19. Mailed a credit memorandum to E. Stern for return of defective merchandise sold him on account for $65.   19.____

20. The proprietor, John Walker, drew $90 cash for personal use.   20.____

21. Received a money order for $110 from B. Kiner for invoice of merchandise charged to him.   21.____

22. Mr. Walker, proprietor, drew $1,200 from his personal savings account and invested the entire sum in his business. 22.____

23. Issued check to Clark & Co. in payment of invoice amounting to $500. Discount of 3% was taken. 23.____

24. Received a 30-day non-interest bearing note for $610 from A. Allen for merchandise sold him today. 24.____

25. Sent a check for $51 to Collector of Internal Revenue for Social Security Taxes collected for the past three months. 25.____

Questions 26-35.

DIRECTIONS: Below you will find the General Journal used by D. Prince, wholesaler. Under the heading of each money column you will find a letter of the alphabet. Following the General Journal, there is a series of transactions. You are to determine the correct entry for each transaction and then show in the appropriate space at the right the columns to be used.
 For example: If a certain transaction results in an entry of $100 in the Notes Receivable Column (on the left side) and an entry of $100 in the General Ledger Column (on the right side), in the appropriate space at the right you should write A, D.
 If the record of the transaction requires the use of more than two columns, your answer should contain more than two letters.
 Do not put the amounts on your answer space. The letters of the columns to be used are sufficient.
 If a transaction requires no entry in the General Journal, write "None" in the appropriate space at the right, even though a record would be made in some other journal.

GENERAL JOURNAL

Notes Rec.	Accts. Pay.	General Ledger	L. F.		General Ledger	Accts. Rec.	Notes Payable
A	B	C			D	E	F

26. Issued a credit memorandum for $68 to J. Winston for goods returned to us. 26.____

27. P. Jones sent us his 60-day note for $750 in full settlement of his account. 27.____

28. Sent a 60-day note to J. O'Connor for invoice of $375 less 2%. 28.____

29. H. Owens sent us a credit memorandum for overcharge of $75 on invoice. 29.____

30. Mailed a 30-day draft to W. Kinder, a customer, for his acceptance amounting to $375 for invoice of goods sold him yesterday. 30.____

31. A. Hocker, a customer, went out of business owing us $170. The claim is considered worthless. 31._____

32. The proprietor requested the bookkeeper to provide a reserve of $500 for expected losses on customers' accounts. 32._____

33. P. Winston sent us a $350 bank draft in full settlement of his account. 33._____

34. Accepted a 30-day trade acceptance drawn by A. Hall for bill of goods amounting to $316 purchased by us last week. 34._____

35. Mr. D. Prince, the proprietor, takes his brother, L. Prince, into the business as an equal partner. Mr. L. Prince invests merchandise worth $3,500 in the business and becomes a partner. 35._____

Questions 36-50.

DIRECTIONS: Below you will find a list of accounts from the ledger of R. Lincoln. There is a letter of the alphabet before each account.
Using the letter in front of each account title (using no accounts not listed), make journal entries for the transactions given below.
Do not write the names of the accounts in your answer space. Simply indicate in the proper space at the right the letters of the accounts to be debited or credited.
Always give the letter or letters of accounts to be debited first, then give the letter or letters of accounts to be credited.
For example, if Office Supplies and Delivery Expenses are to be debited and Notes Payable and Cash are to be credited in a certain transaction, then write as your answer L, D; K, C.

A. Accounts Payable
B. Accounts Receivable
C. Cash
D. Delivery Expense
E. Discount on Purchases
F. Freight Inward
G. Interest Cost
H. Purchases
I. Notes Receivable

J. Notes Receivable Discounted
K. Notes Payable
L. Office Supplies
M. R. Lincoln, Personal
N. Petty Cash
O. Purchase Returns
P. Sales Discount
R. Sales Returns
S. Sales Income

36. Paid the Fox Transportation Co. $15 by check for express charges on goods delivered to us. 36._____

37. Accepted a 30-day trade acceptance for $850 drawn on us by Allen & Co. 37._____

38. Returned damaged goods to H. Parker and he sent us a credit memorandum for $47. 38._____

39. John Smith's 30-day note for $800, which was discounted by us at our bank last month, was paid by him today.   39.____

40. Paid our 60-day note due today in favor of S. Paul for $600 with interest. The check amounted to $606.   40.____

41. The total of the Notes Payable column in the General Journal amounted to $450 at the end of last month. It was posted in error to the Notes Receivable Discounted account. Make the correction entry.   41.____

42. Issued a check to J. News in settlement of invoice $500 less 2%.   42.____

43. Paid Stern Stationers $5.00 by check for four reams of paper for office use.   43.____

44. Sent a check for $48 to Gregory's Garage for storage, gasoline, oil, and service on auto trucks.   44.____

45. Drew a check for $100 to establish a Petty Cash fund.   45.____

46. A. Black, a customer, settled his account of $400 by sending us a check for $100 and a 30-day note for the balance.   46.____

47. J. Walters failed to deduct a discount of $10 when he paid us last month. He called the matter to our attention and we sent him a check for $10.   47.____

48. Donated to the Salvation Army merchandise out of stock costing the proprietor $75.   48.____

49. At the end of the year, the Sales Returns account had a balance of $225. make the entry to close this account.   49.____

50. At the end of the year, the Freight Inward account had a balance of $450. Make the entry to close this account.   50.____

Questions 51-60.

DIRECTIONS: In answering Questions 51 through 60, print the CORRECT answer in the space at the right.

51. On December 31, a bookkeeper prepared a Profit and Loss Statement in which the following are some of the items listed: 51.____
    Sales $50,000
    Purchases   45,000
    Inventory (Jan. 1)   7,500
    Sales Returns   400
    Gross Profit   15,000
    Selling expense   3,200
Find the Inventory of Merchandise on December 31.

52. A. Landers invested $5,000 in cash in a new business. At the end of the year, he finds he has $2,500 in cash, $1,000 in furniture, $1,800 in merchandise on which he owes $750. During the year, Mr. Landers drew $2,400 for his own use. What was his profit or loss for the year? (Write P or L before the figure.)

52._____

53. Wm. Abbott purchased a machine for $2,800. The estimated life of the machine was five years. At the end of five years, the machine could be sold for scrap for $400. Find the depreciation charge at the end of the first six months of use.

53._____

54. On January 1, A. Menton's Capital was $2,400. His partner, P. King, had a Capital of $6,000. Their agreement provided for dividing profits in proportion to Capital. During the year the Net Profit was $12,480. What was A. Menton's share of the Net Profit?

54._____

55. On December 31, J. Klein's ledger, after all closing entries, contained the following balances:

Cash	$5,000
Merchandise Inventory	1,500
Accounts Receivable	8,000
Notes Receivable	2,000
Deferred Expense	300
Furniture and Fixtures	1,200
Accounts Payable	4,000
Reserve for Bad Debts	600
Notes Receivable Discounted	800
Reserve for Depreciation of Furniture and Fixtures	900

What was J. Klein's Capital on December 31?

55._____

56. An employer paid $160 in Social Security taxes at the rate of 1% on taxable wages. He expects to employ more persons next year and pay out 50% more in taxable wages than he did. What will be his Social Security costs at the new rate of 1½% next year?

56._____

57. On June 17, you discounted a customer's 60-day note at your bank. The face of the note was $840 and it was dated June 5, discount rate 6%. What was the amount of the net proceeds?

57._____

58. On June 18, you sold I. Cohen, of Chicago, merchandise. The invoice totaled $684, which included $38 freight which you had prepaid. Terms were 2, 10, n/30, f.o.b. New York. If Mr. Cohen pays you on June 27, what should be the CORRECT amount of the check?

58._____

59. A bankrupt firm agrees to pay its creditors 30 cents on the dollar. It pays Klein & Co. $12,600. What was Klein & Co.'s loss?

59._____

60. A salesman earned $15,600 in one year. His commissions were at the rate of 7½% of sales. What were his sales for the year?   60.____

Questions 61-80.

DIRECTIONS: Questions 61 through 80 are to be answered on the basis of the following:
   The bookkeeper of Walters Co. began to make a trial balance of his General Ledger on December 31. Before he had completed his trial balance, you were permitted to examine his work.
   If a balance is in the correct column, print "C" in the appropriate space at the right. If a balance is in the wrong column, print "W" in the appropriate space at the right.
   Caution: Since the trial balance is not complete, do not attempt to strike a balance of the figures given in the question.

WALTER CO.
Trial Balance, December 31

61.	Merchandise, Inventory, Jan. 1	16,000		61.____
62.	Freight Inward	150		62.____
63.	Petty Cash		75	63.____
64.	Interest Income	70		64.____
65.	Notes Receivable	4,000		65.____
66.	Sales		17,000	66.____
67.	Sales Discount		170	67.____
68.	Purchase Returns	250		68.____
69.	Auto Trucks	9,000		69.____
70.	Reserve for Depreciation of Furniture	770		70.____
71.	Bad Debts		160	71.____
72.	Sales Taxes Collected	225		72.____
73.	Sales Returns		485	73.____
74.	Reserve for Bad Debts		500	74.____
75.	Deposits with Landlord		150	75.____

76. Accrued Interest on Notes Receivable   50   76.____
77. Income from Commissions   900   77.____
78. Purchase Discounts   110   78.____
79. Depreciation of Furniture   225   79.____
80. Notes and Acceptances from Customers   780   80.____

KEY (CORRECT ANSWERS)

1.	C, E	21.	B, E	41.	J; K	61.	C
2.	F, H, I, K	22.	A, E	42.	A; C, E	62.	C
3.	B, D, E	23.	G, J, K	43.	L; C	63.	W
4.	None	24.	None	44.	D; C	64.	W
5.	F, K	25.	F, K	45.	N; C	65.	C
6.	G, K	26.	C, E	46.	I, C; B	66.	C
7.	F, K	27.	A, E	47.	P; C	67.	W
8.	A, E	28.	B, D, F	48.	M; H	68.	W
9.	F, K	29.	B, D	49.	H; F	69.	C
10.	B, E	30.	None	50.	H; F	70.	W
11.	A, E	31.	C, E	51.	17900	71.	W
12.	F, K	32.	C, D	52.	P1950	72.	W
13.	None	33.	None	53.	220	73.	W
14.	A, D, E	34.	B, F	54.	3565.71	74.	C
15.	A, E	35.	C, D	55.	11700	75.	W
16.	F, K	36.	F; C	56.	360	76.	W
17.	None	37.	A; K	57.	833.28	77.	C
18.	F, K	38.	A; O	58.	671.08	78.	C
19.	None	39.	J; K	59.	29400	79.	W
20.	F, K	40.	K, G; C	60.	208000	80.	W

TEST 2

DIRECTIONS: Each question or incomplete statement is followed by several suggested answers or completions. Select the one that BEST answers the question or completes the statement. *PRINT THE LETTER OF THE CORRECT ANSWER IN THE SPACE AT THE RIGHT.*

Questions 1-25.

DIRECTIONS: Below you will find:
1. General Ledger balances on January 31, appearing in books of A. New.
2. All entries on books of A. New for month of February
3. You are to supply balances of ledger accounts on February 29, in the appropriate spaces at the right, as indicated at the end of these questions.

The correct balances in A. New's General Ledger on January 31 were as follows: Cash $7,642; Notes Receivable $2,600; Accounts Receivable $3,100; Furniture and Fixtures $750; Delivery Equipment $1,200; Purchases $2,850; Telephone and Telegrams $110; Office Supplies $380; Salaries $300; Sales Discount $80; Purchase Discount $56; Insurance $160; Sales $3,150; Freight Inward $70; Accounts Payable $2,400; Freight Outward (debit) $40; Notes Payable $1,100; A. New Capital $12,200; A. New Personal (credit) $310; Sales Taxes Payable $35; Withholding Taxes Payable $28; and Social Security Taxes Payable $3.

CASH RECEIPTS

Date	Name	Net Cash	Sales Disc.	Accts. Rec.	Miscellaneous Account	Amount
2/2	S. Wilson	471.00	9.00	480.00		
2/5	First Nat'l Bank	500.00			Notes Pay.	500.00
2/16	M. Tower	350.00			Notes Rec.	340.00
					Int. Income	10.00
2/20	Paul Smith	245.00	5.00	250.00		
2/28	Sundry Customers	110.00			Sales	110.00
	TOTALS	$1675.00	$14.00	$730.00		$960.00

CASH DISBURSEMENTS

Date	Name	Net Cash	Purch. Disc.	Soc. Sec. Tax	With-hold. Taxes	Accts. Pay.	Miscellaneous Account	Amount
2/3	Sun Realty Co.	125					Rent	125
2/9	Bell Smith Co.	540	10			550		
2/10	First Nat'l Bank	808					Notes Pay.	800
							Int. Cost	8
2/14	James Roe Co.	1360	22			1382		
2/16	Roxy Desk Co.	125					Fur. & Fixt.	125
2/20	Baldwin Auto	1650					Del. & Equip.	1650
2/28	Payroll	360		4	36		Sal.	400
2/28	A. New	215					A. New Pers.	215
	TOTALS	$5183	32	4	36	1932		3323

21

2 (#2)

SALES BOOK

Date	Name	Accts. Rec.	Sales	Freight Out	Sales Tax
2/2	Booth &White	460.00	455.00	5.00	
2/10	Water & Co.	375.00	364.00	11.00	
2/14	Neville Bros.	204.00	200.00		4.00
2/16	A. Parker	918.00	900.00		18.00
	TOTALS	$1957.00	1919.00	16.00	22.00

PURCHASE BOOK

Date	Name	Accts. Payable	Purchases	Freight Inward	Miscellaneous Account	Amount
2/4	Walden Co.	800.00	800.00			
2/5	Power Telephone	17.00			Tel.	17.00
2/9	Mfgs. Ins. Co.	122.00			Insurance	122.00
2/12	Tower & Co.	756.00	748.00	8.00		
2/16	X-cel Express	13.00		13.00		
2/23	Braver & Co.	265.00	265.00			
2/28	Penn Stationers	65.00			Off. Suppl.	65.00
	TOTALS	$2038.00	1813.00	21.00		204.00

Supply the balances of the following accounts on February 29, after all posting has been done for February. Print the answers in the appropriate spaces at the right. (Give amounts only.)

1. Cash   1._____
2. Notes Receivable   2._____
3. Accounts Receivable   3._____
4. Furniture and Fixtures   4._____
5. Delivery Equipment   5._____
6. Purchases   6._____
7. Telephone   7._____
8. Office Supplies   8._____
9. Salaries   9._____
10. Sales Discount   10._____
11. Purchase Discount   11._____
12. Insurance   12._____

3 (#2)

13. Freight Inward   13.____
14. Sales   14.____
15. Accounts Payable   15.____
16. Freight Outward   16.____
17. Notes Payable   17.____
18. A. New, Capital   18.____
19. A. New, Personal   19.____
20. Sales Taxes Payable   20.____
21. Withholding Taxes Payable   21.____
22. Social Security Taxes Payable   22.____
23. Interest Income   23.____
24. Rent   24.____
25. Interest Cost   25.____

Questions 26-50.

DIRECTIONS: Below is a list of some of the accounts containing balances in the ledger of the Ajax Company on December 31st after posting all entries for the year, except adjusting and closing entries.
   If the account normally would have a debit balance, write "D" in the proper numbered space at the right. If the amount normally would have a credit balance, write "C" in the proper numbered space at the right.

26. Notes Receivable   26.____
27. Merchandise Inventory   27.____
28. Notes Payable   28.____
29. Interest on Notes Receivable   29.____
30. Freight Inward   30.____
31. Sales Discount   31.____
32. Samuel Ajax Proprietor   32.____

4 (#2)

33. Purchase Returns and Allowances 33.____
34. Land and Buildings 34.____
35. Reserve for Depreciation of Furniture and Fixtures 35.____
36. Purchase Discount 36.____
37. Rent Collected from Sub-Tenants 37.____
38. Taxes Accrued 38.____
39. Notes Receivable Discounted 39.____
40. Accounts Payable 40.____
41. Interest on Notes Payable 41.____
42. Sales Returns and Allowances 42.____
43. Reserve for Bad Debts 43.____
44. Income from Commissions 44.____
45. Deposits from Customers on Containers 45.____
46. Sales 46.____
47. Accounts Receivable 47.____
48. United States Government Bonds 48.____
49. Sales Taxes Collected 49.____
50. Deposit with Gas Company 50.____

Questions 51-90.

DIRECTIONS: As an employee for Wallace and Pace, you have taken a trial balance of the General Ledger on December 31. After posting all adjusting entries but before closing the accounts, you find your adjusted trial balance is correct. You are now requested to prepare a classified balance sheet using only the following classifications:
    A. Current Assets
    B. Fixed Assets
    C. Deferred Charges
    D. Current Liabilities
    E. Fixed Liabilities
    F. Capital

5 (#2)

Indicate the balance sheet classification of the following items by putting the letter (A to F) in the corresponding spaces at the right. However, if any of the following items should *not* appear in our classified balance sheet, write the letter "P" in the corresponding space at the right.

51. Cash   51._____
52. Furniture and Fixtures   52._____
53. Notes Receivable   53._____
54. Reserve for Bad Debts   54._____
55. Merchandise Inventory 1/1   55._____
56. Freight In   56._____
57. A. Wallace, Capital   57._____
58. Sales Returns   58._____
59. Notes Payable   59._____
60. Purchase Discount   60._____
61. Reserve for Depreciation of Furniture and Fixtures   61._____
62. Insurance Unexpired   62._____
63. Interest Cost   63._____
64. Salaries   64._____
65. Shipping Supplies Inventory as of 12/31   65._____
66. Accounts Receivable   66._____
67. Bad Debts   67._____
68. Shipping Supplies   68._____
69. Mortgage Payable   69._____
70. Depreciation on Furniture and Fixtures   70._____
71. L. Pace, Personal (credit)   71._____
72. Land, Buildings   72._____

73. Depreciation on Buildings 73.____
74. Interest Accrued on Notes Receivable 74.____
75. Petty Cash Fund 75.____
76. Taxes 76.____
77. Sales Discount 77.____
78. Merchandise Inventory 12/31 78.____
79. Sales 79.____
80. Interest Income 80.____
81. Purchases 81.____
82. Insurance 82.____
83. Accounts Payable 83.____
84. Salaries Accrued 84.____
85. Reserve for Depreciation of Buildings 85.____
86. Taxes Payable 86.____
87. Purchase Returns 87.____
88. Interest Accrued on Mortgage 88.____
89. A. Wallace, Personal (debit) 89.____
90. L. Pace, Capital 90.____

Questions 91-110.

DIRECTIONS: Below you will find a list of accounts with a number before each:
1. Accounts Payable
2. Accounts Receivable
3. Cash
4. Freight Inward
5. Freight Outward
6. Interest Cost
7. Interest Income
8. Notes Payable
9. Notes Receivable
10. Notes Receivable Discounted
11. Petty Cash Fund
12. Proprietor's Capital Account
13. Purchases
14. Purchase Discounts
15. Purchase Returns
16. Real Estate
17. Sales
18. Sales Discounts
19. Selling Expenses
20. Selling Expenses

7 (#2)

Using the number in front of each account, make journal entries for the transactions listed below.

Do not write the names of the accounts in your answer space. Simply indicate in the proper space at the right the numbers of the accounts to be debited or credited. Always give the number of the account to be debited first, then give the number of the account to be credited.

Example: If Cash is to be debited and Sales is to be credited, write as your answer 3-17.

91. Drew a check to establish a Petty Cash Fund. 91._____

92. A. Paul, a customer, sent us a 60-day interest-bearing note for an invoice previously entered on our books. 92._____

93. Sent a credit memorandum to a customer for goods returned to us. 93._____

94. Our bank notified us that a customer's check was returned marked "insufficient funds." 94._____

95. Accepted a 60-day draft drawn on us by a creditor for invoice previously entered on the books. 95._____

96. A customer sent us a check as a deposit on goods to be sent him. 96._____

97. Issued a certified check for the purchase of real estate. 97._____

98. Received notice from the bank that our account was charged for the payment of trade acceptance given to a creditor two months ago. 98._____

99. Returned merchandise to a creditor and received a credit memorandum. 99._____

100. Sent a check to a customer whose account had been overpaid in error. 100._____

101. The proprietor invested additional cash in the business. 101._____

102. Received a bank draft from a customer in payment of a note. 102._____

103. Sent our 90-day interest-bearing note to a creditor in settlement of account. 103._____

104. Honored a sight draft drawn on us by one of our creditors. 104._____

105. Sold goods to a customer, terms 60 days. 105._____

106. A customer's note, which we had discounted two months ago, was collected by our bank. 106._____

107. Purchased merchandise, terms 2/10 E.O.M. 107._____

108. Paid our note today. 108._____

109. A customer notifies us that he failed to deduct a discount on his last remittance. Sent him a check for the discount. 109._____

110. Last month's total of the Accounts Receivable column in the Cash Receipts book was posted in error to Notes Receivable Account. Make the correction entry. 110._____

Questions 111-112

DIRECTIONS: Questions 111 and 112 are to be answered based on the following:

T. Lawson uses controlling accounts and a card system for the individual accounts with his customers and creditors.
The card containing the account with G. White, to whom he sells goods, has been lost. Reference to monthly schedules of Accounts Receivable shows that White owed $3500 on April 1; $2900 on May 1; and $4300 on June 1.
The cash book shows that Lawson received the following payments from White: $2500 on April 7; $3400 on April 14; and $3800 on May 25.
The journal shows that damaged goods were returned by White on April 15, $250, and that White received an allowance of $50 for shortages on May 16. White gave Lawson a note for $3200 on May 30.

111. What were the Sales to White during April? 111._____

112. What were the Sales to White during May? 112._____

Questions 113-114

DIRECTIONS: Questions 113 and 114 are to be answered on the basis of the following:

Your cash book balance on July 31 was $9242.18.
The bank statement sent to you on August 1 shows a credit for interest of $16.20 and a deduction of $4.50 for collection expenses.
You discover that one check paid by the bank was made out for $78.29 and you had entered it in the cash book as $72.89.
The checks outstanding are #235 for $409.08; #240 for $279; #241 for $42.10; and #247 for $913.56.

113. What balance did the bank report? 113._____

114. What was your true cash balance on August 1? 114._____

115. You received an invoice dated Sept. 5, terms 2/10, n/30, f.o.b. destination, amounting to $350. The shipper paid $25 freight. On Sept. 8 you received a credit memorandum for $15 worth of goods returned. What was the amount of the check required to pay the invoice on Sept. 14? 115._____

116. On March 3 you drew a check to pay an invoice of $750, terms 2/10, E.O.M., dated Feb. 3. What was the amount of the check?   116.____

117. On March 14 you drew a check to pay an invoice of $460, which included $30 freight prepaid by shipper. Invoice dated March 6 carried items 5/10, n/60. What was the amount of the check?   117.____

118. March 15 – Your employer borrowed from his bank on his own 90-day note for $1400. Rate of discount 6%. What amount should you enter in your net cash column in your cash receipts book?   118.____

119. May 9 – You discounted a customer's 60-day note at your bank. Face of note was $480. Date of note was May 3rd. Discount rate was 6%. What was the amount of the net proceeds?   119.____

120. Your Dec. 31 trial balance contained an item for Interest Income $165. On that date you discovered that you had collected $15 interest in advance, and that there was $22 interest accrued on customers' notes not yet due. What amount should be listed on the year's Profit and Loss Statement as interest income?   120.____

KEY (CORRECT ANSWERS)

1.	4135	26.	D	51.	A	76.	P	101.	3-12
2.	2260	27.	D	52.	B	77.	P	102.	3-9
3.	4327	28.	C	53.	A	78.	A	103.	1-8
4.	875	29.	C	54.	A	79.	P	104.	1-3
5.	2850	30.	D	55.	P	80.	P	105.	2-17
6.	4663	31.	D	56.	P	81.	P	106.	10-9
7.	127	32.	C	57.	F	82.	P	107.	13-1
8.	445	33.	C	58.	P	83.	D	108.	8-3
9.	700	34.	D	59.	D	84.	D	109.	18-3
10.	94	35.	C	60.	P	85.	B	110.	9-2
11.	88	36.	C	61.	B	86.	D	111.	5550
12.	282	37.	C	62.	A	87.	P	112.	8450
13.	91	38.	C	63.	P	88.	D	113.	10892.41
14.	5179	39.	C	64.	P	89.	F	114.	9248.48
15.	2506	40.	C	65.	A	90.	F	115.	328.30
16.	24	41.	D	66.	A	91.	11-3	116.	735
17.	800	42.	D	67.	P	92.	9-2	117.	438.50
18.	12200	43.	C	68.	P	93.	19-2	118.	1379
19.	95	44.	C	69.	E	94.	2-3	119.	475.68
20.	57	45.	C	70.	P	95.	1-8	120.	172
21.	64	46.	C	71.	F	96.	3-2		
22.	7	47.	D	72.	B	97.	16-3		
23.	10	48.	D	73.	P	98.	8-3		
24.	125	49.	C	74.	A	99.	1-15		
25.	8	50.	D	75.	A	100.	2-3		

BOOKKEEPING PROBLEMS
EXAMINATION SECTION
TEST 1

DIRECTIONS: Each question or incomplete statement is followed by several suggested answers or completions. Select the one that BEST answers the question or completes the statement. *PRINT THE LETTER OF THE CORRECT ANSWER IN THE SPACE AT THE RIGHT.*

1. The accounts in a general ledger are BEST arranged 1.____

    A. in numerical order
    B. according to the frequency with which each account is used
    C. according to the order in which the headings of the columns in the cash journals are arranged
    D. according to the order in which they are used in preparing financial statements

2. A physical inventory is an inventory obtained by 2.____

    A. an actual count of the items on hand
    B. adding the totals of the stock record cards
    C. deducting the cost of goods sold from the purchases for the period
    D. deducting the purchases from the sales for the period

3. Modern accounting practice favors the valuation of the inventories of a going concern at 3.____

    A. current market prices, if higher than cost
    B. cost or market, whichever is lower
    C. estimated selling price
    D. probable value at forced sale

4. A subsidiary ledger contains accounts which show 4.____

    A. details of contingent liabilities of undetermined amount
    B. totals of all asset accounts in the general ledger
    C. totals of all liability accounts in the general ledger
    D. details of an account in the general ledger

5. A statement of the assets, liabilities, and net worth of a business is called a 5.____

    A. trial balance
    B. budget
    C. profit and loss statement
    D. balance sheet

6. The one of the following which is NEVER properly considered a negotiable instrument is a(n) 6.____

    A. invoice
    B. bond
    C. promissory note
    D. endorsed check

7. The term *current assets* USUALLY includes such things as 7.____

    A. notes payable
    B. machinery and equipment
    C. furniture and fixtures
    D. accounts receivable

31

8. An accounting system which records revenues as soon as they are earned and records liabilities as soon as they are incurred regardless of the date of payment is said to operate on a(n) _____ basis.

    A. accrual   B. budgetary   C. encumbrance   D. cash

8.___

9. A *trial balance* is a list of

    A. the credit balances in all accounts in a general ledger
    B. all general ledger accounts and their balances
    C. the asset accounts in a general ledger and their balances
    D. the liability accounts in a general ledger and their balances

9.___

10. A controlling account contains the totals of

    A. the accounts used in preparing the balance sheet at the end of the fiscal period
    B. the individual amounts entered in the accounts of a subsidiary ledger during the fiscal period
    C. all entries in the general journal during the fiscal period
    D. the accounts used in preparing the profit and loss statement for the fiscal period

10.___

11. The ESSENTIAL nature of an asset is that it(s)

    A. must be tangible
    B. must be easily converted into cash
    C. must have value
    D. cost must be included in the profit and loss statement

11.___

12. When an asset is depreciated on the straight-line basis, the amount charged off for depreciation

    A. is greater in the earlier years of the asset's life
    B. is greater in the later years of the asset's life
    C. varies each year according to the extent to which the asset is used during the year
    D. is equal each full year of the asset's life

12.___

Questions 13-27.

    DIRECTIONS: Questions 13 to 27 consist of a list of some of the accounts in a general ledger. Indicate whether each account listed generally contains a debit or a credit balance by putting the letter D (for debit balance) or the letter C (for credit balance) in the correspondingly numbered space on the right for each account listed. For example, for the account Cash, which generally contains a debit balance, you would give the letter D as your answer.

13. Sales Taxes Collected   13.___

14. Social Security Taxes Paid by Employer   14.___

15. Deposits from Customers   15.___

16. Freight Inward   16.___

17. Sales Discount   17.___

18. Withholding Taxes Payable   18.____
19. L. Norton, Drawings   19.____
20. Office Salaries   20.____
21. Merchandise Inventory   21.____
22. L. Norton, Capital   22.____
23. Purchases Returns   23.____
24. Unearned Rent Income   24.____
25. Reserve for Bad Debts   25.____
26. Depreciation of Machinery   26.____
27. Insurance Prepaid   27.____

Questions 28-42.

DIRECTIONS: Questions 28 to 42 consist of a list of some of the accounts in a general ledger. For the purpose of preparing financial statements, each of these accounts is to be classified into one of the following five major classifications, lettered A to E, as follows:
A. Assets   B. Liabilities   C. Proprietorship
D. Income   E. Expense

You are to indicate the classification to which each account belongs by printing the correct letter, A, B, C, D, or E, in the correspondingly numbered space on the right. For example, for the account Furniture and Fixtures, which is an asset account, you would print the letter A.

28. Notes Receivable   28.____
29. Sales   29.____
30. Wages Payable   30.____
31. Office Salaries   31.____
32. Capital Stock Authorized   32.____
33. Goodwill   33.____
34. Capital Surplus   34.____
35. Office Supplies Used   35.____
36. Interest Payable   36.____
37. Prepaid Rent   37.____
38. Interest Cost   38.____
39. Accounts Payable   39.____

40. Prepaid Insurance   40.____

41. Merchandise Inventory   41.____

42. Interest Earned   42.____

43. A trial balance will NOT indicate that an error has been made in   43.____

    A. computing the balance of an account
    B. entering an amount in the wrong account
    C. carrying forward the balance of an account
    D. entering an amount on the wrong side of an account

44. Many business firms maintain a book of original entry in which all bills to be paid are   44.____
    recorded.
    This book is known as a

    A. purchase returns journal   B. subsidiary ledger
    C. voucher register   D. notes payable register

45. Many business firms provide a petty cash fund from which to pay for small items in order 45.____
    to avoid the issuing of many small checks.
    If this fund is replenished periodically to restore it to its original amount, the fund is called
    a(n) _____ fund.

    A. imprest   B. debenture
    C. adjustment   D. expense reserve

46. A firm which voluntarily terminates business, selling its assets and paying its liabilities, is   46.____
    said to be in

    A. receivership   B. liquidation
    C. depletion   D. amortization

47. The phrase *3%-10 days* on an invoice ORDINARILY means that   47.____

    A. 3% of the amount must be paid each 10 days
    B. the purchaser is entitled to only ten days credit
    C. a discount of 3% will be allowed for payment in 10 days
    D. the entire amount must be paid in 10 days or a penalty of 3% of the amount due
       will be added

48. The CHIEF disadvantage of *single-entry* bookkeeping is that it   48.____

    A. is too difficult to operate
    B. is illegal for income tax purposes
    C. provides no possibility of determining net profits
    D. furnishes an incomplete picture of the business

49. Sales *minus* cost of goods sold *equals*   49.____

    A. net profit   B. gross sales
    C. gross profit   D. net sales

50. The amounts of the transactions recorded in a journal are transferred to the general ledger accounts by a process known as

    A. auditing   B. balancing   C. posting   D. verifying

51. A merchant purchased a stock of goods and priced these goods so as to gain 40% on the cost to him.
    If the merchant sold these goods for $840, the COST of these goods to him was

    A. $556   B. $600   C. $348   D. $925

52. In the interest at 6% for one full year on a principal sum amounts to $12, the *principal sum* is

    A. $150   B. $96   C. $196   D. $200

53. On October 17, a business man discounted a customer's 90-day non-interest bearing note at his bank. The face of the note was $960, and it was dated September 28. The discount rate was 5%.
    Using a 360-day year, the amount in cash that the business man received from the bank was MOST NEARLY

    A. $899.33   B. $950.67   C. $967.50   D. $989.75

54. A certain correctly totaled cash receipts journal contained the following columns: Net Cash Debit, Accounts Receivable, Sales Discounts, and General.
    At the end of April, the totals of the columns were as follows: Net Cash Debit - $18,925.15, Accounts Receivable (not given), Sales Discounts - $379.65, General - $5,639.25.
    The TOTAL of the Accounts Receivable column was

    A. $11,194.50   B. $21,344.32   C. $7,621.19   D. $13,665.55

55. In its first year of operation, a retail store had cash sales of $49,000 and installment sales of $41,000.
    If 12% of the amount of these installment sales were collected in that year, the TOTAL amount of cash received from sales was

    A. $22,176   B. $34,987   C. $53,920   D. $55,650

56. I. Conklin and J. Ulster formed a partnership and agreed to share profits in proportion to their initial capital investments. I. Conklin invested $15,000 and J. Ulster invested $12,500.
    If the profits for the year were $16,500, J. Ulster's share of the profits was

    A. $6,750   B. $7,500   C. $8,100   D. $8,300

57. In a certain city, the tax rate on real estate one year was $48.75 per thousand dollars of assessed valuation. If an apartment house in that city was assessed for $185,000, the real estate tax payable by the owner of that house was MOST NEARLY

    A. $9,018.75   B. $9,009.75   C. $8,900.00   D. $8,905.25

58. A correctly totaled cash payments journal contained the following columns: Net Cash, Accounts Payable, Purchase Discounts, General.
At the end of April, the totals of the columns were as follows: Net Cash - $18,375.60, Accounts Payable - $16,981.19, Purchase Discounts (not given), General - $1,875.37.
The TOTAL of the Purchase Discounts column was

    A. $120.36   B. $239.87   C. $480.96   D. $670.51

58.____

59. On January 1, the credit balance of the Accounts Payable account in a general ledger was $9,139.87. For the month of January, the Purchase Journal total amounted to $3,467.81; the Accounts Payable column in the Cash Disbursements Journal amounted to $2,935.55; the total of the Returned Purchases Journal for January amounted to $173.15; and the Miscellaneous column in the Cash Disbursements Journal showed that $750 had been paid in January on notes given to creditors and entered in previous months.
The BALANCE in the Accounts Payable account at the end of January was

    A. $8,437.89   B. $9,498.98   C. $9,998.98   D. $10,132.68

59.____

60. The bank statement received from his bank by a business man showed a certain balance for the month of June. This bank statement showed a service charge of $5.19 for the month. He discovered that a check drawn by him in the amount of $83.75 and returned by the bank had been entered on the stub of his checkbook as $38.75. He also found that two checks which he had issued, #29 for $37.18 and #33 for $18.69, were not listed on the statement and had not been returned by the bank. The balance in his checkbook before he reconciled it with the balance shown on the bank statement was $8,917.91.
The BALANCE on the bank statement was

    A. $8,903.97   B. $8,923.59   C. $8,997.65   D. $9,303.95

60.____

KEY (CORRECT ANSWERS)

1.	D	16.	D	31.	E	46.	B		
2.	A	17.	D	32.	C	47.	C		
3.	B	18.	C	33.	A	48.	D		
4.	D	19.	D	34.	C	49.	C		
5.	D	20.	D	35.	E	50.	C		
6.	A	21.	D	36.	B	51.	B		
7.	D	22.	C	37.	A	52.	D		
8.	A	23.	C	38.	E	53.	B		
9.	B	24.	C	39.	B	54.	D		
10.	B	25.	C	40.	A	55.	C		
11.	C	26.	D	41.	A	56.	B		
12.	D	27.	D	42.	D	57.	A		
13.	C	28.	A	43.	B	58.	C		
14.	D	29.	D	44.	C	59.	B		
15.	C	30.	B	45.	A	60.	B		

TEST 2

Questions 1-25.

DIRECTIONS:
1. Below you will find the general ledger balances on February 28 in the books of C. Dutton.
2. On the following pages, you will find all the entries on the books of C. Dutton for the month of March.
3. In the appropriate spaces on the right, you are to supply the new balances for the accounts called for at the end of March.

The correct balances in the general ledger of C. Dutton on February 28 were as follows: (NOTE: The accounts below have not been arranged in the customary trial balance form.)

Cash	$4,336
Accounts Receivable	8,165
Notes Receivable	2,200
Furniture and Fixtures	9,000
Merchandise Inventory 1/1	4,175
Accounts Payable	5,560
Notes Payable	1,500
Reserve for Depreciation of Furniture and Fixtures	1,800
C. Dutton, Capital	14,162
C. Dutton, Drawing	900
Purchases	42,600
Freight In	36
Rent	1,750
Light	126
Telephone	63
Salaries	4,076
Shipping Expenses	368
Sales	53,200
Sales Biscount	637
Purchase Biscount	596
City Sales Tax Collected	804
Social Security Taxes Payable	96
Withholding Taxes Payable	714

CASH RECEIPTS

Date	Name	Net Cash	Accounts Receivable	Sales Disc.	Miscellaneous Acct.	Amount
3/1	T. Blint	6,027.00	6,150.00	123.00		
	K. Crowe	1,015.00			Notes Rec.	1,000.00
					Int. Income	15.00
3/10	N. Tandy	3,969.00	4,050.00	81.00		
3/17	Rebuilt Desk Co.	45.00			Furn. & Fixt.	45.00
3/24	J. Walter	2,910.00	3,000.00	90.00		
3/31	National Federal Bank	3,000.00			Notes Payable	3,000.00
		16,966.00	13,200.00	294.00		4,060.00

37

2 (#2)

CASH DISBURSEMENTS

Date		Net Cash	Accts. Pay.	Purch. Disc.	Soc. Sec. Tax	With-hold Tax	Miscellaneous Acct.	Amount
3/1	Bliss Realty Co.	875.00					Rent	875.00
3/4	Con. Edison	54.00					Light	54.00
3/10	D. LaRue	2,891.00	2,950.00	59.00				
3/15	Payroll	747.00			26.00	175.	Sal.	948.00
3/19	Rebuilt Desk Co.	115.00					Furn/Fixt	115.00
3/26	Jiggs & Co.	3,686.00	3,800.00	114.00				
3/30	Nat'l Fed Bank	1,218.00					Notes Pay.	1200.00
							Int. Cost	18.00
3/31	Payroll	733.00			22.00	171.	Salary	926.00
3/31	C. Dutton	600.00					Draw	600.00
		10,919.00	6,750.00	173.00	48.00	346.00		4736.00

SALES BOOK

Date	Name	Accts. Rec.	Sales	City Sales Tax
3/3	K. Crowe	6,850.00	6,665.00	185.00
3/10	J. Walters	5,730.00	5,730.00	
3/16	N. Tandy	3,100.00	3,007.00	93.00
3/25	Willis & Co.	7,278.00	7,069.00	209.00
3/30	V. Clyburne	2,190.00	2,190.00	
		25,148.00	24,661.00	487.00

PURCHASE BOOK

Date		Accts. Pay.	Purchases	Freight In	Miscellaneous Acct.	Amount
3/4	Jiggs & Co.	5,212.00	5,070.00	142.00		
3/11	Barton & Co.	320.00			Ins. Prepd.	320.00
3/16	A. Field	6,368.00	6,179.00	189.00		
3/19	Smith Delivery	22.00			Ship. Exp.	22.00
3/23	N.Y. Telephone	29.00			Telephone	29.00
3/26	D. LaRue	3,000.00	3,000.00			
3/29	App & App	7,531.00	7,168.00	363.00		
		22,482.00	21,417.00	694.00		371.00

Supply the balances of the following accounts on March 31 after all posting has been done for March. Put answers in the appropriate spaces on the right. Give amounts only.

1. Cash   1.____
2. Accounts Receivable   2.____
3. Notes Receivable   3.____
4. Insurance Prepaid   4.____
5. Furniture and Fixtures   5.____
6. Accounts Payable   6.____
7. Notes Payable   7.____

8. Reserve for Depreciation of Furniture and Fixtures   8.____
9. C. Dutton, Capital   9.____
10. C. Dutton, Drawing   10.____
11. Purchases   11.____
12. Freight In   12.____
13. Rent   13.____
14. Light   14.____
15. Telephone   15.____
16. Salaries   16.____
17. Shipping Expenses   17.____
18. Sales   18.____
19. Sales Discount   19.____
20. Purchase Discount   20.____
21. City Sales Tax Collected   21.____
22. Social Security Taxes Payable   22.____
23. Withholding Taxes Payable   23.____
24. Interest Income   24.____
25. Interest Cost   25.____

Questions 26-35.

DIRECTIONS: Mr. Adams has a complete set of books - Cash Journals, Purchase and Sales Journals, and a General Journal. Below you will find the General Journal used by Mr. Adams. Under the heading of each money column, you will find a letter of the alphabet. Following the General Journal, there is a series of transactions. You are to determine the correct entry for each transaction and then show on the right in the appropriate space the columns to be used. For example, if a certain transaction results in an entry of $100 in the Notes Receiving Column (on the left side) and an entry of $100 in the General Ledger Column (on the right side), in the appropriate space on the right, you should write A, D. If the record of the transaction requires the use of more than two columns, your answer should contain more than two letters. DO NOT PUT THE AMOUNTS IN YOUR ANSWER SPACE. The LETTERS of the columns to be used are sufficient. If a transaction requires no entry in the General Journal, write *None* in the appropriate space in your answer space, even though a record would be made in some other journal.

GENERAL JOURNAL

Notes Receivable	Accounts Payable	General Ledger	L. F.		General Ledger	Accounts Receivable	Notes Payable
A	B	C			D	E	F

26. We sent Tripp & Co. a 30-day trade acceptance for $500 for merchandise sold him today. They accepted it.   26.____

27. The proprietor, Mr. Adams, returned $100 in cash to be deposited, representing Traveling Expenses he had not used.   27.____

28. An entry in the purchase journal last month for a purchase invoice from V. Valides for $647 was erroneously entered in the purchase journal as $746 and posted as such.   28.____

29. A check for $200 received from Mr. Breen was erroneously credited to account of P. Ungar.   29.____

30. In posting the totals of the cash receipts journal last month, an item of bank discount of $30 on our note for $1500 discounted for 60 days was included in the total posted to the sales discount account.   30.____

31. M. Hogan paid his note of $600 and interest of $12 and his account was credited for $612.   31.____

32. Mr. Blow informed us he could not pay his invoice of $2000 due today. Instead, he sent us his 30-day note for $2000 for 30 days bearing interest at 6% per annum.   32.____

33. The proprietor, Mr. Adams, drew $75 to buy his daughter a U.S. Bond.   33.____

34. Mr. O'Brien wrote to us that we overcharged him on an invoice last week.   34.____

35. Returned $120 worth of merchandise to Pecora & Co. and received their credit memorandum.   35.____

Questions 36-50.

DIRECTIONS: In Questions 36 to 50, you will find a list of accounts with a number before each.

1. Cash
2. Accounts Receivable
3. Notes Receivable
4. Notes Receivable Discounted
5. Furniture and Fixtures
6. Delivery Equipment
7. Insurance Prepaid
8. Depreciation on Delivery Equipment
9. Bad Debts
10. Purchases
11. Discount on Purchases
12. Sales
13. Discount on Sales
14. Accounts Payable
15. Notes Payable
16. Interest Cost
17. Reserve for Depreciation on Delivery Equipment
18. Reserve for Bad Debts
19. Sales Taxes Collected
20. Ben Miller, Capital
21. Ben Miller, Drawing
22. Interest Income
23. Purchase Returns

Using the number in front of each account title (using no accounts not listed), make journal entries for the transactions given below. Do not write the names of the accounts in your answer space. Simply indicate in the proper space on the right the numbers of the accounts to be debited or credited. Always give the number or numbers of the accounts to be debited first, then give the number or numbers of accounts to be credited. For example, if furniture and fixtures and delivery equipment are to be debited, and cash and notes payable are to be credited in a certain transaction, then write in your answer space 5, 6 - 1, 15 (use a dash to separate the debits from the credits).

36. F. Pierce, a customer, went into bankruptcy owing us $600. We received a check for $200. 36.____

37. Later in the month, we are informed that there is no possibility of collecting the balance from F. Pierce. There is a sufficient balance in the Reserve for Bad Debts to take care of the above. 37.____

38. Set up the Depreciation on the Delivery Equipment for the year amounting to $240. 38.____

39. Discounted M. Colby's note for $500 today and received $490 in proceeds. 39.____

40. Mr. Miller, the proprietor, invested $2000 in the business. 40.____

41. Paid our note due to Dillon & Co. today for $800 with interest of $16. 41.____

42. Accepted Finnegan's trade acceptance for $1500 for merchandise bought today. 42.____

43. Create a Reserve for Bad Debts of $2000 at the end of the year. 43.____

44. Returned to Dillon & Co. $30 worth of damaged merchandise for credit. They allowed it. 44.____

45. G. Garry claimed a discount of $12 which we had failed to allow him. He had already paid his bill. Sent him check for $12. 45.____

46. On one sale during the month, we had failed to collect the Sales Tax of $15. Wrote to the customer and he sent us a check for $15. 46.____

47. M. Colby paid his note due today which we had discounted two months ago. 47.____

48. Bought a new safe for $875 from Cramer & Co., terms 2/10, n/60 days. Agreed to pay them in 60 days. 48.____

49. Bought merchandise during the month amounting to $17,500 - all on account. 49.____

50. On December 31, paid for a Fire Insurance policy to run for three years from that date - premium was $480. 50.____

51. The following information was taken from the ledger of Peter Dolan on Dec. 31 after adjusting entries had been posted to the ledger. 51.____

Sales Income	$60,000
Sales Returns	3,500
Mdse. Purchases	42,000
Inventory of 1/1	9,400
Sales Taxes Payable	360
Freight Inward	225
Inventory 12/31	7,640
Insurance Unexpired	163

Find the gross profit on Sales for the year.

52. On March 31, your bank sent you a statement of account. You compared the canceled checks with the stubs in your checkbook and found the following:

   Check #34 - $56.00 had not been paid by the bank
   #44 - $38.00 had been paid by the bank as $38.89 because the amount on the check did not agree with your stub in the checkbook
   #52 - $76.50 had not been returned by the bank, though the check had been certified
   #57 - $127.42 had not been paid by the bank

   What total amount would you deduct from the balance on the bank's statement as checks outstanding?

52.___

53. On April 30, Mr. Jolley received his statement of account from the bank. A comparison of the bank statement and your checkbook revealed the following: Checkbook balance $5,640; this included a deposit of $325 on the last day of April which had not been entered on the bank statement.
   You also find the following:

   Check #69 - $89.00 had not been paid by the bank
   #70 - Paid by the bank as $47.55, had been entered in your checkbook as $45.57
   #76 - $114.30 had not been paid by the bank

   The bank statement included a debit memo of $4.00 for excessive activity during the month.
   What was the balance on the bank statement?

53.___

54. An invoice dated January 15 for merchandise you bought added up to $876.00. The terms were 3/10, n/60, F.O.B. DESTINATION. When the goods arrived, you paid freight amounting to $8.50. On January 20, you returned goods billed at $26 and received credit therefor. You paid the bill on January 24.
   What was the amount of your check?

54.___

55. Income taxes paid by residents of a certain state are based on the balance of taxable income at the following

   rates: 2% on first $1000 or less
   3% on 2nd and 3rd $1000
   4% on 4th and 5th $1000
   5% on 6th and 7th $1000
   6% on 8th and 9th $1000
   7% on all over $9000

   What would be the NORMAL income tax to be paid by a resident of that state whose taxable balance of income was $6,750?

55.___

56. A salesman's gross earnings for the year came to $8,820. His rate of Commission was 5% of his sales to customers after deducting returns by customers. During the year, his customers returned 10% of the goods they purchased. What were his total sales during the year before deducting returns?

56.___

57. On December 31, the insurance account contained a debit for $144 for a three-year fire insurance policy dated August 1. What amount should be listed on the balance sheet of December 31 of that year?

57.___

58. A partnership began business on January 1 with partners' investments of $26,000. During the year, the partners drew $18,500 for personal use. On December 31, the assets of the firm were $46,300, and the liabilities were $15,600. What was the firm's net profit for the year? (Write P or L before your answer.) 58.____

59. The rent income account of a real estate firm showed a total balance of $75,640 at the end of 1986. Of this amount, $3,545 represented prepaid 1987 rents. The account also included entries for 1986 rents due from tenants but not yet collected, amounting to $2,400.
What amount should be listed on the profit and loss statement as rent income for 1986? 59.____

60. You discounted a customer's note for $7,200 at your bank at the rate of 6% and received net proceeds of $7,182.
How many days did the note have to run from date of discount to date of maturity? (Use 360 days to the year.) 60.____

Questions 61-90.

DIRECTIONS: In Questions 61 to 90, you will find a list of ledger accounts. Indicate whether an account is generally listed in the Trial Balance as a DEBIT or as a CREDIT by putting the letter *D* or the letter *C* in the correct space on the right for each account listed.

61. Sales   61.____
62. Land   62.____
63. Notes Payable   63.____
64. Traveling Expenses   64.____
65. Purchases   65.____
66. Buildings   66.____
67. Merchandise Inventory   67.____
68. Machinery and Equipment   68.____
69. Notes Receivable   69.____
70. Bonds Payable   70.____
71. Advertising   71.____
72. Delivery Expense   72.____
73. Cash   73.____

8 (#2)

74. Accounts Payable   74.____
75. Interest on Bonds   75.____
76. Real Estate Taxes   76.____
77. Accounts Receivable   77.____
78. Don Burch, Proprietor   78.____
79. Sales Discount   79.____
80. Withholding Taxes   80.____
81. Depreciation   81.____
82. Prepaid Insurance   82.____
83. Reserve for Dep. on Buildings   83.____
84. Rent Income   84.____
85. Reserve for Bad Debts   85.____
86. Don Burch, Drawing Account   86.____
87. Sales Returns   87.____
88. Bad Debts   88.____
89. Purchase Discount   89.____
90. Reserve for Dep. on Machinery & Equipment   90.____

KEY (CORRECT ANSWERS)

1.	$ 10,383	31.	C,D,D	61.	C
2.	$ 20,113	32.	A,E	62.	D
3.	$ 1,200	33.	None	63.	C
4.	$ 320	34.	C,E	64.	D
5.	$ 9,070	35.	B,D	65.	D
6.	$ 21,292	36.	1-2	66.	D
7.	$ 3,300	37.	18-2	67.	D
8.	$ 1,800	38.	8-17	68.	D
9.	$ 14,162	39.	1,16-4	69.	D
10.	$ 1,500	40.	1-20	70.	C
11.	$ 64,017	41.	15,16-1	71.	D
12.	$ 730	42.	14-15	72.	D
13.	$ 2,625	43.	9-18	73.	D
14.	$ 180	44.	14-23	74.	C
15.	$ 92	45.	13-1	75.	D
16.	$ 5,950	46.	1-19	76.	D
17.	$ 390	47.	4-3	77.	D
18.	$ 77,861	48.	5-14	78.	C
19.	$ 931	49.	10-14	79.	D
20.	$ 769	50.	7-1	80.	C
21.	$ 1,291	51.	$12,515	81.	D
22.	$ 144	52.	$ 183.42	82.	D
23.	$1,060	53.	$ 5,512.32	83.	C
24.	$ 15	54.	$ 816	84.	C
25.	$ 18	55.	$ 247.50	85.	C
26.	A-E	56.	$196,000	86.	D
27.	None	57.	$ 124	87.	D
28.	B-D	58.	P $23,200	88.	D
29.	C,E	59.	$72,095	89.	C
30.	C,D	60.	15	90.	C

TEST 3

DIRECTIONS: Each question or incomplete statement is followed by several suggested answers or completions. Select the one that BEST answers the question or completes the statement. *PRINT THE LETTER OF THE CORRECT ANSWER IN THE SPACE AT THE RIGHT.*

1. Of the following taxes, the one which is levied MOST NEARLY in accordance with ability to pay is a(n) _____ tax.

    A. excise
    B. income
    C. general property
    D. sales

2. When a check has been lost, the bank on which it is drawn should ORDINARILY be notified and instructed to

    A. stop payment on the check
    B. issue a duplicate of the check
    C. charge the account of the drawer for the amount of the check
    D. certify the check

3. The profit and loss statement prepared for a retail store does NOT ordinarily show

    A. the cost of goods sold
    B. depreciation of fixtures and equipment
    C. expenditures for salaries of employees
    D. the net worth of the proprietor

4. When two business corporations join their assets and liabilities to form a new corporation, the procedures is called a(n)

    A. merger
    B. liquidation
    C. receivership
    D. exchange

5. The method of depreciation which deducts an equal amount each full year of an asset's life is called _____ depreciation.

    A. sum-of-years digits
    B. declining balance
    C. straight-line
    D. service-hours

6. A fixed asset is an asset that

    A. is held primarily for sale to customers
    B. is used in the conduct of the business until worn out or replaced
    C. is readily convertible into cash
    D. has no definite value

7. The gross profit on sales for a period is determined by

    A. subtracting the cost of goods sold from the sales
    B. subtracting the sales returns and the discounts on sales from the gross sales
    C. subtracting the sales from the purchases for the period
    D. finding the difference between the inventory of merchandise at the beginning of the period and the inventory of merchandise at the end of the period

8. The term *auditing* refers to the

   A. entering of amounts from the journals into the general ledger
   B. reconciliation of the accounts in a subsidiary ledger with the controlling account in the general ledger
   C. preparation of a trial balance of the accounts in the general ledger
   D. examination of the general ledger and other records of a concern to determine its true financial condition

9. A voucher register is a

   A. type of electric cash register
   B. list of customers whose accounts are past due
   C. list of the assets of a business
   D. book in which bills to be paid are recorded

10. The account DISCOUNT ON PURCHASES is *properly* closed directly to the _____ account.

    A. Accounts Payable
    B. Sales
    C. Purchases
    D. Fixtures

11. The account UNEARNED RENTAL INCOME is *usually* considered a(n) _____ account.

    A. asset   B. nominal   C. capital   D. liability

12. A controlling account is an account which contains

    A. the totals of *all* the expense accounts in the general ledger
    B. the total of the amounts entered in the accounts in a subsidiary ledger
    C. the total of the depreciation on fixtures claimed in *all* preceding years
    D. *all* totals of the income and expense accounts before closing to the Profit and Loss account

13. The purpose of the DRAWING account in the general ledger of an individual enterprise is to show the

    A. salaries paid to the employees
    B. amounts paid to independent contractors for services rendered
    C. amounts taken by the proprietor for his personal use
    D. total of payments made for general expenses of the business

14. The phrase *2%/10 net 30 days* on an invoice ORDINARILY means that

    A. 2% of the amount must be paid within 30 days
    B. the purchaser must add 2% to the amount of the invoice if he fails to pay within 30 days
    C. the entire amount must be paid within 30 days
    D. the purchaser may deduct 2% from the amount if he pays within 30 days

15. The ESSENTIAL characteristic of a C.O.D. sale of merchandise is that the

    A. purchaser pays for the merchandise upon its receipt by him
    B. seller guarantees the merchandise to be as specified by him
    C. merchandise is delivered by a common carrier
    D. purchaser is permitted to pay for the merchandise in convenient installments

16. If the drawer of a check makes an error in writing the amount of the check, he should 16.___

    A. erase the error and insert the correct amount
    B. cross out the error and insert the correct amount
    C. destroy the check and prepare another one
    D. write the correct amount directly above the incorrect one

17. States do NOT levy a(n) _____ tax. 17.___

    A. unemployment insurance   B. income
    C. corporation franchise   D. export

18. The cost of goods sold by a retail store is PROPERLY determined by 18.___

    A. *adding* the closing inventory to the total of the opening inventory and the purchases for the year
    B. *deducting* the closing inventory from the total of the opening inventory and the purchases for the year
    C. *deducting* the total of the opening and closing inventories from the purchases for the year
    D. *adding* the total of the opening and closing inventories

19. The PRIMARY purpose of a trial balance is to determine 19.___

    A. that all transactions have been entered in the journals
    B. the accuracy of the totals in the general ledger
    C. the correctness of the amounts entered in the journals
    D. that amounts have been posted to the proper accounts in the general ledger

20. The SURPLUS account of a corporation is *ordinarily* used to record 20.___

    A. the actual amount subscribed by stockholders
    B. the amount of profits earned by the corporation
    C. any excess of current assets over current liabilities
    D. the total of the fixed assets of the corporation

Questions 21-30.

DIRECTIONS: Each of Questions 21 to 30 consists of a typical transaction of Our Business followed by the debit and credit (amounts omitted) of the journal entry for that transaction. For each of these questions, the debit and credit given may be appropriately classified under one of the following categories:

   A. The debit of the journal entry is CORRECT but the credit is INCORRECT.
   B. The debit of the journal entry is INCORRECT but the credit is CORRECT.
   C. BOTH the debit and the credit of the journal entry are correct.
   D. BOTH the debit and the credit of the journal entry are incorrect.

Examine each question carefully. Then, in the correspondingly numbered space on the right, mark as your answer the letter preceding the category which is the BEST of the four suggested above.

SAMPLE QUESTION: We purchased a desk for cash.
   Debit: Office Equipment
   Credit: Accounts Payable

In this example, the debit is correct but the credit is incorrect. Therefore, you should mark A as your answer.

21. We sent a check for $500 to R. Thomas in payment for an invoice for that amount.   21.____
    Debit: Cash   Credit: Accounts Receivable

22. We took merchandise, amounting to $35, for our own use.   22.____
    Debit: Proprietor, Personal   Credit: Purchases

23. Arthur Townsend's 90-day note for $350, which was discounted by us at our bank last month, was paid by him today.   23.____
    Debit: Notes Receivable Discounted
    Credit: Accounts Receivable

24. We sold merchandise to T. Wilson on account of $275.   24.____
    Debit: Accounts Payable   Credit: Sales

25. We returned damaged merchandise to B. Lowell and received a credit memorandum from him for $28.   25.____
    Debit: Accounts Payable
    Credit: Sales Returns and Allowances

26. We paid our 30-day note given to Mr. Kane for $650 without interest.   26.____
    Debit: Notes Receivable   Credit: Cash

27. We sent Chet Carr a check for $10.50 for a discount he had forgotten to take when he paid us for merchandise this week.   27.____
    Debit: Sales Discounts   Credit: Cash

28. The bank loaned us $1000, and we invested it in the business.   28.____
    Debit: Cash   Credit: Loan Receivable

29. We recorded depreciation for the year on our office equipment.   29.____
    Debit: Reserve for Depreciation of Office Equipment
    Credit: Depreciation of Office Equipment

30. One of our customers, Allen Koren, was declared bankrupt and his debt of $25 to us was canceled.   30.____
    Debit: Reserve for Bad Debts Credit: Accounts Receivable

Questions 31-45.

DIRECTIONS: Questions 31 to 45 consist of a list of some of the accounts in the general ledger of a corporation which operates a retail store. Indicate whether each account listed contains generally a debit or credit balance by marking the letter D (for debit balance) or the letter C (for credit balance) in the correspondingly numbered space on the right.
For example, for the account Cash, which generally contains a debit balance, you would mark the letter D as your answer.

31. Rent Expense   31.___
32. Allowance for Depreciation of Fixtures   32.___
33. Sales Returns and Allowances   33.___
34. Security Deposit for Electricity   34.___
35. Accrued Salaries Payable   35.___
36. Dividends Payable   36.___
37. Petty Cash Fund   37.___
38. Notes Receivable Discounted   38.___
39. Surplus   39.___
40. Capital Stock Authorized   40.___
41. Insurance Expense   41.___
42. Sales for Cash   42.___
43. Purchase Discounts   43.___
44. Automobile Delivery Equipment   44.___
45. Bad Debts Expense   45.___

Questions 46-60.

DIRECTIONS: Questions 46 to 60 consist of a list of some of the accounts in a general ledger. For the purpose of preparing financial statements, each of these accounts is to be classified into one of the following five major classifications, lettered A to E, as follows:
A. Assets   B. Liabilities   C. Income   D. Expense   E. Capital You are to indicate the classification to which each belongs by marking the appropriate letter, A, B, C, D or E. in the correspondingly numbered space on the right. For example, for the account MERCHANDISE INVENTORY, which is an asset account, you would mark the letter A as your answer.

46. Purchases   46.___
47. Prepaid Interest   47.___
48. Cash in Bank   48.___
49. Depreciation of Fixtures   49.___

50. Accounts Receivable   50.____
51. Mortgage Payable   51.____
52. Accrued Interest Receivable   52.____
53. Bad Debts   53.____
54. Insurance Expired   54.____
55. Treasury Stock   55.____
56. Investments   56.____
57. Loan to Partner   57.____
58. Unearned Rent Received   58.____
59. Petty Cash Fund   59.____
60. Loss on Sale of Equipment   60.____

KEY (CORRECT ANSWERS)

1.	B	16.	C	31.	D	46.	D
2.	A	17.	D	32.	C	47.	A
3.	D	18.	B	33.	D	48.	A
4.	A	19.	B	34.	D	49.	D
5.	C	20.	B	35.	C	50.	A
6.	B	21.	D	36.	C	51.	B
7.	A	22.	C	37.	D	52.	A
8.	D	23.	A	38.	C	53.	D
9.	D	24.	B	39.	C	54.	D
10.	C	25.	A	40.	C	55.	E
11.	D	26.	B	41.	D	56.	A
12.	B	27.	C	42.	C	57.	A
13.	C	28.	A	43.	C	58.	B
14.	C	29.	D	44.	D	59.	A
15.	A	30.	C	45.	D	60.	D

EXAMINATION SECTION
TEST 1

DIRECTIONS: Each question or incomplete statement is followed by several suggested answers or completions. Select the one that BEST answers the question or completes the statement. *PRINT THE LETTER OF THE CORRECT ANSWER IN THE SPACE AT THE RIGHT.*

Questions 1-7.

DIRECTIONS: Questions 1 through 7 are to be answered on the basis of the following income statement.

Laura Lee's Bridal Shop
Income Statement
For the Year Ended December 31, 2018

Revenue:		
New & Used Bridal Gowns & Accessories		$55,000
Expenses:		
Advertisement Expense	$ 2,000	
Salaries Expense	12,000	
Dry cleaning & Alterations	10,000	
Utilities	1,500	
Total Expenses		25,500
Net Income		$29,500

1. What is the period of time covered by this income statement?　　1.____

   A. January-December 2017
   B. December 2018
   C. January 2017-December 2018
   D. January-December 2018

2. What is the source of the revenue?　　2.____

   A. New and used bridal gowns, advertisements, salaries, dry cleaning, and utilities
   B. Advertisements, salaries, dry cleaning, alterations, and utilities
   C. New and used bridal gowns and accessories
   D. Net income

3. What is the total revenue?　　3.____

   A. $25,500   B. $55,000   C. $29,500   D. $79,500

4. Which of the following are expenses?　　4.____

   A. Salaries
   B. New and used bridal gowns and accessories
   C. Revenue
   D. New and used bridal gowns, advertisements, and dry cleaning

5. What are the total expenses?　　5.____

   A. $55,000   B. $29,500   C. $79,500   D. $25,500

6. There is a resulting net income because 6.____

   A. total revenue and total expenses are combined
   B. net income is greater than total revenue
   C. the total revenue is greater than total expenses
   D. the total revenue is less than total expenses

7. Is this statement an interim statement? 7.____

   A. Yes, because it covers an entire accounting period
   B. No, because it covers an entire accounting period
   C. Yes, because it covers a period of less than a year
   D. No, because it covers a period of more than a year

8. What is the name of the accounting report that may show either a net profit or a net loss for an accounting period? 8.____

   A. Income statement   B. Balance sheet
   C. Statement of capital   D. Classified balance sheet

9. What are the two main parts of the body of the income statement? 9.____

   A. Cash and Capital   B. Revenue and Expenses
   C. Liabilities and Capital   D. Assets and Notes Payable

10. If total revenue exceeds total expenses for an accounting period, what is the difference called? 10.____

    A. Gross income   B. Total liabilities
    C. Total assets   D. Net income

11. In the body of a balance sheet, what are the three sections called? 11.____

    A. Assets and liabilities
    B. Cash, liabilities, and revenue
    C. Assets, liabilities, and capital
    D. Revenue, assets, and capital

12. What business record shows the results of the proprietor's borrowing assets from the business, usually in anticipation of profits? 12.____

    A. Proprietor's withdrawals
    B. Accounts payable
    C. Liabilities and Capital
    D. Total liabilities

Questions 13-24.

DIRECTIONS: For each transaction given for Mona's Magic Moments Hair Salon in Questions 13 through 24, identify which journal the transaction should be recorded in.

13. April 1: Mona, the owner, paid the month's rent - $600.00; check no. 356. 13.____

    A. General   B. Cash disbursements
    C. Purchases   D. Sales

14. April 6: the salon purchased $300.00 worth of styling products on account from Pomme de Terre Company.   14.____

    A. Cash disbursements B. General
    C. Sales   D. Purchases

15. April 8: sold $100.00 worth of hair products on account to Mrs. Angela Bray.   15.____

    A. Sales   B. Purchases
    C. Cash disbursements D. General

16. April 11: the owner, Mona Ramen, withdrew $80.00 of styling products for personal use.   16.____

    A. Sales   B. Cash receipts
    C. General D. Cash disbursements

17. April 13: paid Pomme de Terre Company $300.00 on account; check 357.   17.____

    A. Purchases   B. Cash disbursements
    C. Cash receipts D. General

18. April 15: cash sales to date were $4,607.00.   18.____

    A. Cash disbursements B. Purchases
    C. Sales   D. General

19. April 17: issued credit slip #17 to Mrs. Angela Bray for $25.00 for merchandise returned.   19.____

    A. Cash disbursements B. Cash receipts
    C. Sales   D. General

20. April 19: paid electric bill for $250.00; check no. 358.   20.____

    A. Cash disbursements B. Purchases
    C. General   D. Cash receipts

21. April 21: received $75.00 from Mrs. Angela Bray for balance due on account.   21.____

    A. Sales   B. Cash disbursements
    C. Cash receipts D. Purchases

22. April 23: sold $88.00 of hair products on account to Ms. Tania Alioto.   22.____

    A. Purchases   B. Sales
    C. Cash disbursements D. Cash receipts

23. April 27: purchased $500.00 of equipment from Salon Stylings Merchandisers on account.   23.____

    A. Cash disbursements B. Sales
    C. General   D. Purchases

24. April 30: cash sales to date were $5023.00.   24.____

    A. Purchases   B. Sales
    C. Cash receipts D. General

Questions 25-30.

DIRECTIONS: Questions 25 through 30 are to be answered on the basis of the following ledger for a barbecue take-out restaurant owned and operated by Ruby Joiner.

```
      Cash              Accounts Receivable    Delivery Equipment
450 | 150              360 | 170               5,000 |
212 | 125              250 | 100               4,000 |
328 | 440              165 | 120               3,000 |
172 | 125              100 |  60
250 |  70
275 | 150
325 |  50

    Supplies           Ruby Joiner, Capital     Accounts Payable
40 |                        | 8,200            10 | 600
65 |                        | 2,000            15 | 300
30 |                        | 2,097               | 200
25 |

Ruby Joiner, Drawing      Advertising Expense    Delivery Income
225 |                     40 |                       | 400
175 |                     45 |                       | 350
200 |                                                | 250
                                                     | 100

Trucking Expense          Telephone Expense
100 |                     80 |
 50 |                     40 |
                          20 |
```

25. What is the balance on the Cash account shown above?

    A. 2,012.00   B. 1,110.00   C. 3,122.00   D. 902.00

26. What is the balance on the Accounts receivable account shown above?

    A. 425.00   B. 875.00   C. 450.00   D. 1315.00

27. What is the balance on the Accounts payable account shown above?

    A. 1100.00   B. 1075.00   C. 25.00   D. 1125.00

28. Which of the above accounts has a balance of 1100.00?

    A. Accounts payable   B. Delivery Income
    C. Cash   D. Delivery equipment

29. Which of the above accounts has a balance of 12,000.00?

    A. Ruby Joiner, Capital
    B. Cash and Accounts receivable combined
    C. Delivery equipment
    D. None of the accounts

30. If you made a balance sheet out of the information listed above, Ruby Joiner's total assets would be

    A. 14,472.00   B. 12,297.00   C. 13,392.00   D. 13,487.00

Questions 31-34.

DIRECTIONS: Questions 31 through 34 are to be answered on the basis of the following information, to be included on a checking deposit ticket.

Five $20 bills; 11 $10 bills; 6 $5 bills; 47 $1 bills; 200 half dollars; 120 quarters; 112 dimes; 320 nickels; 67 pennies. Second National Bank (73-124) check of 152.34; Bank of the Midwest (13-298) check of 68.37; Great National Bank (32-165) check of 185.06.

31. What is the TOTAL currency for this deposit? 31.____
    A. $387   B. $287   C. $444.87   D. $157.87

32. What is the TOTAL coin for this deposit? 32.____
    A. $387   B. $287   C. $444.87   D. $157.87

33. What is the check total for this deposit? 33.____
    A. $692.77   B. $406   C. $405.77   D. $850.64

34. What is the TOTAL deposit? 34.____
    A. $444.87   B. $692.77   C. $851   D. $850.64

Questions 35-37.

DIRECTIONS: Questions 35 through 37 are to be answered on the basis of the following petty cash journal.

Date	Receipt No.	To Whom Paid	For What	Acct.#	Amount
10/2	1	Anna Jones - Mail	Postage	548	13.50
10/2	2	Jim Collins	Messenger	525	5.75
10/4	3	Anna Jones - Mail	Postage	548	13.50
10/5	4	Lucky Stores	Coffee	515	7.34
10/6	5	Tom Allen	Lunch w/customer	525	11.38

35. What is the TOTAL disbursement from this fund for the time period 10/1 through 10/6? 35.____
    A. $51.47   B. $40.09   C. $61.47   D. $26.59

36. How much money was disbursed to Account #548 during the time period 10/1-10/16? 36.____
    A. $51.47   B. $26   C. $27   D. $34.34

37. If the fund began the month with a total of $100.00, what amount was left in the fund at the end of business on 10/5? 37.____
    A. $48.53   B. $59.91   C. $51.47   D. $40.09

Questions 38-40.

DIRECTIONS: Questions 38 through 40 are to be answered on the basis of the following information.

A promissory note dated December 1, 2018, bearing interest at a rate of 12% and due in 90 days, is sent to a creditor. The face value of the note is $900.

38. What is the due date of the promissory note?   38.____

    A. January 15, 2019   B. March 1, 2019
    C. February 1, 2019   D. December 31, 2018

39. What is the TOTAL interest that will be earned on the note?   39.____

    A. $27   B. $270   C. $108   D. $10.80

40. What interest will be earned on the note for the old accounting period (December 1-31)?   40.____

    A. $90   B. $36   C. $9   D. $3.60

KEY (CORRECT ANSWERS)

1.	D	11.	C	21.	C	31.	B
2.	C	12.	A	22.	B	32.	D
3.	B	13.	B	23.	D	33.	C
4.	A	14.	D	24.	B	34.	D
5.	D	15.	A	25.	D	35.	A
6.	C	16.	C	26.	A	36.	C
7.	B	17.	B	27.	B	37.	B
8.	A	18.	C	28.	B	38.	B
9.	B	19.	D	29.	C	39.	A
10.	D	20.	A	30.	D	40.	C

TEST 2

DIRECTIONS: Each question or incomplete statement is followed by several suggested answers or completions. Select the one that BEST answers the question or completes the statement. *PRINT THE LETTER OF THE CORRECT ANSWER IN THE SPACE AT THE RIGHT.*

Questions 1-4.

DIRECTIONS: Questions 1 through 4 are to be answered on the basis of the following information, to be included in a deposit slip.

    14 twenty dollar bills   63 quarters
    52 ten dollar bills   22 dimes
    12 five dollar bills   44 nickels
    43 one dollar bills   70 pennies

Checks: $236.34 and $129.72

1. What is the TOTAL amount of currency for this deposit?   1.____
   A. $923.85   B. $1269.06   C. $903.00   D. $1299.91

2. What is the TOTAL amount of coin for this deposit?   2.____
   A. $20.85   B. $923.85   C. $903.00   D. $1299.91

3. What is the TOTAL amount of check for this deposit?   3.____
   A. $20.85   B. $366.06   C. $1299.91   D. $903.00

4. What is the TOTAL deposit for this slip?   4.____
   A. $1269.06   B. $903.00   C. $923.85   D. $1289.91

Questions 5-7.

DIRECTIONS: Questions 5 through 7 are to be answered on the basis of the following information.

    Angela Martinez's last check stub balance was $675.50. Her bank statement balance dated April 30 was $652.00. A $250 deposit was in transit on that date. Outstanding checks were as follows: No. 127, $65.00; No. 129, $203.50; No. 130, $50.00. The bank service charge for the month was $5.00.

5. What was Angela Martinez's available checkbook balance on April 30?   5.____
   A. $652.00   B. $338.50   C. $583.50   D. $675.50

6. In order to reconcile her checkbook balance with her bank statement balance, what must Angela Martinez do?   6.____
       A. Add her checkbook balance to the balance on her bank statement
       B. Subtract her checkbook balance from the balance on her bank statement

C. Ignore her checkbook balance and adopt the balance on her bank statement
D. Adjust the checkbook balance by adding deposits and debiting outstanding checks and charges

7. The check stub balance referred to in the problem refers to the 7.____

   A. last check Angela Martinez recorded in her checkbook
   B. amount of money left in Angela Martinez's account according to her own calculations based on the checks, charges, and deposits she has written and recorded
   C. amount of money left in Angela Martinez's account according to the bank's calculations based on the checks, charges, and deposits posted to her account
   D. number of checks left in her checkbook

Questions 8-9.

DIRECTIONS: Questions 8 and 9 are to be answered on the basis of the following information.

Tu Nguyen, an interior designer, received his June bank statement on July 2. The balance was $622.66. His last check stub balance was $700. On comparing the two, he noticed that a deposit of $275 made on June 30 was not included on the statement; also, a bank service charge of $4 was deducted. Outstanding checks were as follows: No. 331, $97.50; No. 332, $207; No. 335, $25.40; and No. 336, $68.97.

8. What is Nguyen's CORRECT available bank balance? 8.____

   A. $494.79   B. $897.66   C. $700.00   D. $219.79

9. The bank statement balance referred to in the problem refers to the 9.____

   A. last check Tu Nguyen recorded in his checkbook
   B. last check presented for payment to Tu Nguyen's account
   C. amount of money left in Tu Nguyen's account according to the bank's calculations based on the checks, charges, and deposits posted to his account
   D. amount of money left in Tu Nguyen's account based on his own calculations of the checks, charges, and deposits he has written and recorded

10. What of the following endorsements would be an example of a simple Endorsement in Blank? 10.____

    A. Pay to the Order of Joanie Anderson
    B. Joanie Anderson
    C. For deposit only; Acct. No. 12345; Joanie Anderson
    D. Without Recourse; Joanie Anderson

11. Which of the following endorsements would limit the further purpose or use of the endorsed check? 11.____

    A. Pay to the Order of Joanie Anderson
    B. Joanie Anderson
    C. For deposit only; Acct. No. 12345; Joanie Anderson,
    D. Without Recourse; Joanie Anderson

12. Which of the following endorsements would protect the endorser from legal responsibility for payment, should the drawer have insufficient funds to honor his/her own check?   12._____

    A. Pay to the Order of Joanie Anderson
    B. Joanie Anderson
    C. For deposit only; Acct. No. 12345; Joanie Anderson
    D. Without Recourse; Joanie Anderson

Questions 13-24.

DIRECTIONS: Questions 13 - 24 are to be answered on the basis of the following ledger accounts for Wheelsmith Organic Farms.

Wheelsmith Organic Farms
Ledger Accounts

Cash	Accounts Payable	Service Supplies
Jan. 1 4,000	Jan. 1 2,000	Jan. 1 2,000

Shelley Wheelsmith, Capital	Machinery
Jan. 1 11,000	Jan. 1 7,000

13. Transaction #1: On January 5, Shelley Wheelsmith, the proprietor, received cash amounting to $5,000 as a result of returning machinery that had recently been purchased. What account(s) should this transaction be posted to?   13._____

    A. Cash
    B. Cash and Machinery
    C. Machinery
    D. Cash, Machinery, and Service Supplies

14. Transaction #2: On January 8, Shelley Wheelsmith, the proprietor, sent out a check for $600 in partial payment of the accounts payable.   14._____
    What account(s) should this transaction be posted to?

    A. Accounts Payable
    B. Accounts Payable and Cash
    C. Accounts Payable and Capital
    D. Cash

15. Transaction #3: On January 14, Shelley Wheelsmith, proprietor, made an additional investment in the business by contributing machinery valued at $1,500.   15._____
    What account(s) should this transaction be posted to?

    A. Machinery   B. Machinery and Capital
    C. Capital   D. Machinery and Cash

16. Transaction #4: On January 26, Shelley Wheelsmith, proprietor, purchased additional service supplies for $200. She agreed to pay the obligation in 30 days. What account(s) should this transaction be posted to?   16._____

A. Accounts Payable and Liabilities
B. Service supplies
C. Accounts Payable
D. Accounts Payable and Service supplies

17. Transaction #5: On January 31, Shelley Wheelsmith, proprietor, purchased service supplies paying cash of $50. What account(s) should this transaction be posted to?   17.____

    A. Service supplies
    B. Service supplies and Accounts Payable
    C. Cash and Service supplies
    D. Cash

18. What is the balance in the Cash account after all of these transactions are posted?   18.____

    A. $9,000   B. $1,000   C. $5,000   D. $8,350

19. What is the balance in the Machinery account after all of these transactions are posted?   19.____

    A. $7,000   B. $5,000   C. $3,500   D. $13,500

20. What is the balance in the Accounts Payable account after all of these transactions are posted?   20.____

    A. $800   B. $600   C. $2,600   D. $1,600

21. What is the balance in the Capital account after all of these transactions are posted?   21.____

    A. $12,500   B. $800   C. $11,600   D. $10,400

22. What is the balance in the Service supplies account after all of these transactions are posted?   22.____

    A. $2,000   B. $2,250   C. $750   D. $2,200

23. What are the total assets of Wheelsmith Organic Farms after these transactions have been posted?   23.____

    A. $10,600   B. $11,850   C. $14,100   D. $10,750

24. What are the total liabilities and capital for Wheelsmith Organic Farms after these transactions have been posted?   24.____

    A. $14,100   B. $12,500   C. $11,850   D. $10,600

Questions 25-28.

DIRECTIONS: Questions 25 through 28 are to be answered on the basis of the following information.

At the end of an accounting period, Andy's Framing Gallery recorded the following information: Sales, $125,225; Merchandise Inventory, December 31, $95,325; Purchases Returns and Allowances, $3,500; Merchandise Inventory, January 1, $98,725; Freight on Purchases, $2,500; Purchases, $120,000.

25. What are the net purchases for Andy's Framing Gallery during the accounting period? 25.____
    A. $120,000   B. $119,000   C. $3,500   D. $122,500

26. What is the cost of goods available for sale? 26.____
    A. $119,000   B. $98,725   C. $95,325   D. $217,725

27. What is the total cost of goods sold for this accounting period? 27.____
    A. $217,725   B. $95,325   C. $122,400   D. $125,225

28. What is the gross profit on sales for this accounting period? 28.____
    A. $2825   B. $2500   C. $125,225   D. $122,400

Questions 29-40.

DIRECTIONS: Questions 29 through 40 are to be answered on the basis of the following information.

The Joie de Vivre Co. received the promissory notes listed below during the last quarter of its calendar year:

	Date	Face Amount	Terms	Interest Rate	Date Discounted	Discount Rate
(1)	10/8	$3,600	30 days	-	10/18	9%
(2)	9/22	$8,000	60 days	6%	10/1	7%
(3)	11/15	$3,000	90 days	7%	11/20	8%

29. What is the due date for the first note? 29.____
    A. 12/31   B. 11/7   C. 12/7   D. 10/31

30. What interest will be due when the first note matures? 30.____
    A. $3   B. $3,600   C. $30   D. $0

31. What is the maturity value of the first note? 31.____
    A. $3,600   B. $3,630   C. $0   D. $3,603

32. What is the discount period for the first note? 32.____
    A. One fiscal year   B. 10 days
    C. 20 days   D. One month

33. What is the due date for the second note? 33.____
    A. 12/21   B. 11/21   C. 10/21   D. 1/21

34. What interest will be due when the second note matures? 34.____
    A. $60   B. $800.00   C. $8.00   D. $80.00

35. What is the maturity value of the second note? 35.____
    A. $8,000   B. $8,080   C. $8,800   D. $8,008

6 (#2)

36. What is the discount period for the second note? 36._____
    A. 51 days   B. 10 days   C. 360 days   D. 60 days

37. What is the due date for the third note? 37._____
    A. 1/14   B. 12/15   C. 12/31   D. 2/13

38. What interest will be due when the third note matures? 38._____
    A. $5.25   B. $52.50   C. $525   D. $90

39. What is the maturity value of the third note? 39._____
    A. $3525   B. $3005.25   C. $3052.50   D. $3090

40. What is the discount period for the third note? 40._____
    A. 60 days   B. 85 days   C. 5 days   D. 90 days

KEY (CORRECT ANSWERS)

1. C	11. C	21. A	31. A
2. A	12. D	22. B	32. C
3. B	13. B	23. C	33. B
4. D	14. B	24. A	34. D
5. C	15. B	25. B	35. B
6. D	16. D	26. D	36. A
7. B	17. C	27. C	37. D
8. A	18. D	28. A	38. B
9. C	19. C	29. B	39. C
10. B	20. D	30. D	40. B

TEST 3

DIRECTIONS: Each question or incomplete statement is followed by several suggested answers or completions. Select the one that BEST answers the question or completes the statement. *PRINT THE LETTER OF THE CORRECT ANSWER IN THE SPACE AT THE RIGHT.*

Questions 1-8.

DIRECTIONS: Questions 1 through 8 are to be answered on the basis of the following Balance Sheet.

Laura Lee's Bridal Shop
Balance Sheet
December 31, 2018

Assets
Cash	$14,000	
Accounts Receivable	3,000	
Bridal Accessories	10,000	
Gowns and Other Inventory	30,000	
Total Assets		$57,000

Liabilities and Capital
Accounts Payable	$ 4,000	
Notes Payable	28,000	
Total Liabilities		$32,000
Laura Lee, Capital		25,000
Total Liabilities and Capital		$57,000

1. When was the balance sheet prepared?

   A. January 2019
   B. December 31, 2018
   C. After the close of the 2018 fiscal year
   D. December 1, 2018

   1._____

2. How does the date on this balance sheet differ from the date on the statement of capital or income statement?

   A. It doesn't differ. The dates for each statement signify the same time period.
   B. The date on a balance sheet represents the period during which any changes indicated on the statement took place, whereas the other financial statements represent the moment in time when the statement was prepared.
   C. The date on a balance sheet represents the moment in time when the statement was prepared, whereas the other financial statements represent the period during which any changes indicated on the statement took place.
   D. The date on a balance sheet indicates an entire year, whereas the dates on the other statements indicate a single month.

   2._____

3. Can Laura Lee purchase more bridal gowns for the business paying cash of $16,000?

   A. *No*, because the business has only $14,000 cash available
   B. *Yes*, because the business has $57,000 cash available
   C. *Yes*, because the business has $57,000 available in assets
   D. *No*, because the business has $57,000 in liabilities

   3._____

65

4. What is the owner's equity of Laura Lee's Bridal Shop? 4._____
   Since total equity consists of total _____, total equity is _____.

   A. assets minus total liabilities and proprietor's capital; $0
   B. assets minus total liabilities; $25,000
   C. assets; $57,000
   D. liabilities and proprietor's capital; $57,000

5. What is the TOTAL amount of Laura Lee's claim against the total assets of the business? 5._____

   A. $57,000   B. $25,000   C. $0   D. $39,000

6. What is the amount of the creditors' claims against the assets of the business? 6._____

   A. $4,000   B. $57,000   C. $32,000   D. $28,000

7. What is the net income for the period? 7._____

   A. $57,000
   B. $0
   C. $25,000
   D. This information cannot be obtained from the balance sheet

8. What was the value of Laura Lee's ownership in this business on January 1, 2004? 8._____

   A. $25,000
   B. $57,000
   C. $14,000
   D. This information cannot be obtained from the balance sheet

Questions 9-21.

DIRECTIONS: Each of the transactions described in Questions 9 through 21 occurred within an accounting period. For each question, indicate which of the four journals the transaction would be recorded in.

9. Sale of goods on account 9._____

   A. Cash receipts   B. Cash payments
   C. General   D. Sales

10. Cash payment of a promissory note 10._____

    A. Cash payments   B. Cash receipts
    C. Sales   D. General

11. Received a credit memo from a creditor 11._____

    A. Purchases   B. General
    C. Sales   D. Cash payments

12. Sale of merchandise for cash 12._____

    A. Purchases   B. General
    C. Cash receipts   D. Cash payments

13. Received a check from a customer in partial payment of an oral agreement   13.____

    A. Purchases   B. Sales
    C. General   D. Cash receipts

14. Issued a credit memo to a customer   14.____

    A. Purchases   B. General
    C. Cash payments   D. Sales

15. Received a promissory note in place of an oral agreement from a customer   15.____

    A. General   B. Cash payments
    C. Cash receipts   D. Sales

16. Paid monthly rent   16.____

    A. General   B. Purchases
    C. Cash payments   D. Cash receipts

17. Sale of a service on credit   17.____

    A. Cash receipts   B. General
    C. Purchases   D. Sales

18. Purchase of office furniture on credit   18.____

    A. General   B. Purchases
    C. Cash payments   D. Cash receipts

19. Purchased merchandise for cash   19.____

    A. Cash payments   B. Cash receipts
    C. Sales   D. General

20. Cash refund to a customer   20.____

    A. Cash receipts   B. Sales
    C. General   D. Cash payments

21. Purchases made on credit   21.____

    A. Purchases   B. Sales
    C. Cash receipts   D. General

Questions 22-26.

DIRECTIONS: Questions 22 through 26 are to be answered on the basis of the following inventory, purchased by International Soap and Candle Traders, Inc.

700 units at $4.50, 320 units at $3.75, 550 units at $2.75, and 475 units at $1.90

22. Calculate the total price of the units that cost $4.50.   22.____

    A. $315   B. $31,500   C. $3,150   D. $2,800

23. Calculate the total price of the units that cost $3.75.   23.____

    A. $2062.50   B. $12,000   C. $120   D. $1,200

24. Calculate the total price of the units that cost $2.75. 24.____

    A. $1,512.50   B. $15,125   C. $151.25   D. $550

25. Calculate the total price of the units that cost $1.90. 25.____

    A. $90.25   B. $9025   C. $902.50   D. $475

26. Calculate the average cost per unit. 26.____

    A. $27   B. $33.10   C. $0.30   D. $3.31

27. The interest on a promissory note is recorded at which of the following times? 27.____

    A. When the debt is incurred
    B. At the end of the accounting period
    C. When the note is paid
    D. At the beginning of each month

28. The interest on a promissory note begins accruing at which of the following times? 28.____

    A. When the debt is incurred
    B. At the end of the accounting period
    C. When the note is paid
    D. At the beginning of each month

29. The maturity value of an interest-bearing note is the 29.____

    A. interest accrued on the note plus a service charge imposed by the lender
    B. interest accrued on the note
    C. face value of the note
    D. principal of the note plus interest

30. A cash receipts journal is used to record the 30.____

    A. number of cash sales a business makes
    B. number of credit sales a business makes
    C. collection of cash made by the business
    D. expenditure of cash made by the business

31. Calculate the interest on a promissory note issued for $3,000 at an interest rate of 8%, due in 360 days. (Assume a banking year of 360 days.) 31.____

    A. $300   B. $240   C. $60   D. $360

32. Calculate the total payment due for a promissory note issued for $1,000 at an interest rate of 10%, due in 90 days. (Assume a banking year of 360 days.) 32.____

    A. $25   B. $1050   C. $1000   D. $1025

33. Calculate the total payment due for a promissory note issued for $5,000 at an interest rate of 6%, due in 60 days. (Assume a banking year of 360 days.) 33.____

    A. $5,050   B. $50   C. $5,000   D. $5,300

34. Calculate the interest on a promissory note issued for $1,700 at an interest rate of 12%, due in 45 days. (Assume a banking year of 360 days.)   34._____

    A. $204   B. $1725.50   C. $25.50   D. $1904

35. Calculate the interest on a promissory note issued for $600 at an interest rate of 9%, due in 90 days. (Assume a banking year of 360 days.)   35._____

    A. $13.50   B. $135   C. $54   D. $540

KEY (CORRECT ANSWERS)

1.	B	16.	C
2.	C	17.	D
3.	A	18.	B
4.	B	19.	A
5.	B	20.	D
6.	C	21.	A
7.	D	22.	C
8.	D	23.	D
9.	D	24.	A
10.	A	25.	C
11.	B	26.	D
12.	C	27.	C
13.	D	28.	A
14.	B	29.	D
15.	A	30.	C

31. B
32. D
33. A
34. C
35. A

RECORD KEEPING
EXAMINATION SECTION
TEST 1

DIRECTIONS: Each question or incomplete statement is followed by several suggested answers or completions. Select the one that BEST answers the question or completes the statement. *PRINT THE LETTER OF THE CORRECT ANSWER IN THE SPACE AT THE RIGHT.*

Questions 1-7.

DIRECTIONS: In answering Questions 1 through 7, use the following master list. For each question, determine where the name would fit on the master list. Each answer choice indicates right before or after the name in the answer choice.

    Aaron, Jane
    Armstead, Brendan
    Bailey, Charles
    Dent, Ricardo
    Grant, Mark
    Mars, Justin
    Methieu, Justine
    Parker, Cathy
    Sampson, Suzy
    Thomas, Heather

1. Schmidt, William
   A. Right before Cathy Parker
   B. Right after Heather Thomas
   C. Right after Suzy Sampson
   D. Right before Ricardo Dent

2. Asanti, Kendall
   A. Right before Jane Aaron
   B. Right after Charles Bailey
   C. Right before Justine Methieu
   D. Right after Brendan Armstead

3. O'Brien, Daniel
   A. Right after Justine Methieu
   B. Right before Jane Aaron
   C. Right after Mark Grant
   D. Right before Suzy Sampson

4. Marrow, Alison
   A. Right before Cathy Parker
   B. Right before Justin Mars
   C. Right before Mark Grant
   D. Right after Heather Thomas

5. Grantt, Marissa
   A. Right before Mark Grant
   B. Right after Mark Grant
   C. Right after Justin Mars
   D. Right before Suzy Sampson

6. Thompson, Heath   6._____
   A. Right after Justin Mars   B. Right before Suzy Sampson
   C. Right after Heather Thomas   D. Right before Cathy Parker

DIRECTIONS: Before answering Question 7, add in all of the names from Questions 1 through 6. Then fit the name in alphabetical order based on the new list.

7. Francisco, Mildred   7._____
   A. Right before Mark Grant   B. Right after Marissa Grantt
   C. Right before Alison Marrow   D. Right after Kendall Asanti

Questions 8-10.

DIRECTIONS: In answering Questions 8 through 10, compare each pair of names and addresses. Indicate whether they are the same or different in any way.

8. William H. Pratt, J.D.   William H. Pratt, J.D.   8._____
   Attourney at Law   Attorney at Law
   A. No differences   B. 1 difference
   C. 2 differences   D. 3 differences

9. 1303 Theater Drive,; Apt. 3-B   1330 Theatre Drive,; Apt. 3-B   9._____
   A. No differences   B. 1 difference
   C. 2 differences   D. 3 differences

10. Petersdorff, Briana and Mary   Petersdorff, Briana and Mary   10._____
    A. No differences   B. 1 difference
    C. 2 differences   D. 3 differences

11. Which of the following words, if any, are misspelled?   11._____
    A. Affordable   B. Circumstansial
    C. Legalese   D. None of the above

Questions 12-13.

DIRECTIONS: Questions 12 and 13 are to be answered on the basis of the following table.

Standardized Test Results for High School Students in District #1230

	English	Math	Science	Reading
High School 1	21	22	15	18
High School 2	12	16	13	15
High School 3	16	18	21	17
High School 4	19	14	15	16

The scores for each high school in the district were averaged out and listed for each subject tested. Scores of 0-10 are significantly below College Readiness Standards. 11-15 are below College Readiness, 16-20 meet College Readiness, and 21-25 are above College Readiness.

12. If the high schools need to meet or exceed in at least half the categories in order to NOT be considered "at risk," which schools are considered "at risk"? 12.____
    A. High School 2   B. High School 3
    C. High School 4   D. Both A and C

13. What percentage of subjects did the district as a whole meet or exceed College Readiness standards? 13.____
    A. 25%   B. 50%   C. 75%   D. 100%

Questions 14-15.

DIRECTIONS: Questions 14 and 15 are to be answered on the basis of the following information.

You have seven employees working as a part of your team: Austin, Emily, Jeremy, Christina, Martin, Harriet, and Steve. You have just sent an e-mail informing them that there will be a mandatory training session next week. To ensure that work still gets done, you are offering the training twice during the week: once on Tuesday and also on Thursday. This way half the employees will still be working while the other half attend the training. The only other issue is that Jeremy doesn't work on Tuesdays and Harriet doesn't work on Thursdays due to compressed work schedules.

14. Which of the following is a possible attendance roster for the first training session? 14.____
    A. Emily, Jeremy, Steve   B. Steve, Christina, Harriet
    C. Harriet, Jeremy, Austin   D. Steve, Martin, Jeremy

15. If Harriet, Christina, and Steve attend the training session on Tuesday, which of the following is a possible roster for Thursday's training session? 15.____
    A. Jeremy, Emily, and Austin   B. Emily, Martin, and Harriet
    C. Austin, Christina, and Emily   D. Jeremy, Emily, and Steve

Questions 16-20.

DIRECTIONS: In answering Questions 16 through 20, you will be given a word and will need to choose the answer choice that is MOST similar or different to the word.

16. Which word means the SAME as *annual*? 16.____
    A. Monthly   B. Usually   C. Yearly   D. Constantly

17. Which word means the SAME as *effort*? 17.____
    A. Energy   B. Equate   C. Cherish   D. Commence

18. Which word means the OPPOSITE of *forlorn*? 18.____
    A. Neglected   B. Lethargy   C. Optimistic   D. Astonished

19. Which word means the SAME as *risk*? 19.____
    A. Admire   B. Hazard   C. Limit   D. Hesitant

20. Which word means the OPPOSITE of *translucent*? 20.____
    A. Opaque   B. Transparent   C. Luminous   D. Introverted

21. Last year, Jamie's annual salary was $50,000. Her boss called her today 21.____
    to inform her that she would receive a 20% raise for the upcoming year. How
    much more money will Jamie receive next year?
    A. $60,000   B. $10,000   C. $1,000   D. $51,000

22. You and a co-worker work for a temp hiring agency as part of their office 22.____
    staff. You both are given 6 days off per month. How many days off are you
    and your co-worker given in a year?
    A. 24   B. 72   C. 144   D. 48

23. If Margot makes $34,000 per year and she works 40 hours per week for 23.____
    all 52 weeks, what is her hourly rate?
    A. $16.34/hour   B. $17.00/hour   C. $15.54/hour   D. $13.23/hour

24. How many dimes are there in $175.00? 24.____
    A. 175   B. 1,750   C. 3,500   D. 17,500

25. If Janey is three times as old as Emily, and Emily is 3, how old is Janey? 25.____
    A. 6   B. 9   C. 12   D. 15

KEY (CORRECT ANSWERS)

1.	C		11.	B
2.	D		12.	A
3.	A		13.	D
4.	B		14.	B
5.	B		15.	A
6.	C		16.	C
7.	A		17.	A
8.	B		18.	C
9.	C		19.	B
10.	A		20.	A

21.	B
22.	C
23.	A
24.	B
25.	B

TEST 2

DIRECTIONS: Each question or incomplete statement is followed by several suggested answers or completions. Select the one that BEST answers the question or completes the statement. *PRINT THE LETTER OF THE CORRECT ANSWER IN THE SPACE AT THE RIGHT.*

Questions 1-6.

DIRECTIONS: Questions 1 through 6 are to be answered on the basis of the following information.

item	name of item to be ordered
quantity	minimum number that can be ordered
beginning amount	amount in stock at start of month
amount received	amount receiving during month
ending amount	amount in stock at end of month
amount used	amount used during month
amount to order	will need at least as much of each item as used in the previous month
unit price	cost of each unit of an item
total price	total price for the order

Item	Quantity	Beginning	Received	Ending	Amount Used	Amount to Order	Unit Price	Total Price
Pens	10	22	10	8	24	20	$0.11	$2.20
Spiral notebooks	8	30	13	12			$0.25	
Binder clips	2 boxes	3 boxes	1 box	1 box			$1.79	
Sticky notes	3 packs	12 packs	4 packs	2 packs			$1.29	
Dry erase markers	1 pack (dozen)	34 markers	8 markers	40 markers			$16.49	
Ink cartridges (printer)	1 cartridge	3 cartridges	1 cartridge	2 cartridges			$79.99	
Folders	10 folders	25 folders	15 folders	10 folders			$1.08	

1. How many packs of sticky notes were used during the month? 1._____
   A. 16   B. 10   C. 12   D. 14

2. How many folders need to be ordered for next month? 2._____
   A. 15   B. 20   C. 30   D. 40

3. What is the total price of notebooks that you will need to order? 3._____
   A. $6.00   B. $0.25   C. $4.50   D. $2.75

4. Which of the following will you spend the second most money on? 4._____
   A. Ink cartridges   B. Dry erase markers
   C. Sticky notes   D. Binder clips

5. How many packs of dry erase markers should you order? 5._____
   A. 1   B. 8   C. 12   D. 0

6. What will be the total price of the file folders you order? 6.____
   A. $20.16 B. $21.60 C. $10.80 D. $4.32

Questions 7-11.

DIRECTIONS: Questions 7 through 11 are to be answered on the basis of the following table.

Number of Car Accidents, By Location and Cause, for 2014						
	Location 1		Location 2		Location 3	
Cause	Number	Percent	Number	Percent	Number	Percent
Severe Weather	10		25		30	
Excessive Speeding	20	40	5		10	
Impaired Driving	15		15	25	8	
Miscellaneous	5		15		2	4
TOTALS	50	100	60	100	50	100

7. Which of the following is the third highest cause of accidents for all three locations? 7.____
   A. Severe Weather
   B. Impaired Driving
   C. Miscellaneous
   D. Excessive Speeding

8. The average number of Severe Weather accidents per week at Location 3 for the year (52 weeks) was MOST NEARLY 8.____
   A. 0.57 B. 30 C. 1 D. 1.25

9. Which location had the LARGEST percentage of accidents caused by Impaired Driving? 9.____
   A. 1 B. 2 C. 3 D. Both A and B

10. If one-third of the accidents at all three locations resulted in at least one fatality, what is the LEAST amount of deaths caused by accidents last year? 10.____
    A. 60 B. 106 C. 66 D. 53

11. What is the percentage of accidents caused by miscellaneous means from all three locations in 2014? 11.____
    A. 5% B. 10% C. 13% D. 25%

12. How many pairs of the following groups of letters are exactly alike? 12.____
    ACDOBJ   ACDBOJ
    HEWBWR   HEWRWB
    DEERVS   DEERVS
    BRFQSX   BRFQSX
    WEYRVB   WEYRVB
    SPQRZA   SQRPZA

    A. 2 B. 3 C. 4 D. 5

Questions 13-19.

DIRECTIONS: Questions 13 through 19 are to be answered on the basis of the following information.

In 2012, the most current information on the American population was finished. The information was compiled by 200 volunteers in each of the 50 states. The territory of Puerto Rico, a sovereign of the United States, had 25 people assigned to compile data. In February of 2010, volunteers in each state and sovereign began collecting information. In Puerto Rico, data collection finished by January 31st, 2011, while work in the United States was completed on June 30, 2012. Each volunteer gathered data on the population of their state or sovereign. When the information was compiled, volunteers sent reports to the nation's capital, Washington, D.C. Each volunteer worked 20 hours per month and put together 10 reports per month. After the data was compiled in total, 50 people reviewed the data and worked from January 2012 to December 2012.

13. How many reports were generated from February 2010 to April 2010 in Illinois and Ohio?
    A. 3,000   B. 6,000   C. 12,000   D. 15,000

14. How many volunteers in total collected population data in January 2012?
    A. 10,000   B. 2,000   C. 225   D. 200

15. How many reports were put together in May 2012?
    A. 2,000   B. 50,000   C. 100,000   D. 100,250

16. How many hours did the Puerto Rican volunteers work in the fall (September-November)?
    A. 60   B. 500   C. 1,500   D. 0

17. How many workers were compiling or reviewing data in July 2012?
    A. 25   B. 50   C. 200   D. 250

18. What was the total amount of hours worked by Nevada volunteers in July 2010?
    A. 500   B. 4,000   C. 4,500   D. 5,000

19. How many reviewers worked in January 2013?
    A. 75   B. 50   C. 0   D. 25

20. John has to file 10 documents per shelf. How many documents would it take for John to fill 40 shelves?
    A. 40   B. 400   C. 4,500   D. 5,000

21. Jill wants to travel from New York City to Los Angeles by bike, which is approximately 2,772 miles. How many miles per day would Jill need to average if she wanted to complete the trip in 4 weeks?
    A. 100   B. 89   C. 99   D. 94

22. If there are 24 CPU's and only 7 monitors, how many more monitors do you need to have the same amount of monitors as CPU's? 22.____
    A. Not enough information B. 17
    C. 31 D. 0

23. If Gerry works 5 days a week and 8 hours each day, and John works 3 days a week and 10 hours each day, how many more hours per year will Gerry work than John? 23.____
    A. They work the same amount of hours.
    B. 450
    C. 520
    D. 832

24. Jimmy gets transferred to a new office. The new office has 25 employees, but only 16 are there due to a blizzard. How many coworkers was Jimmy able to meet on his first day? 24.____
    A. 16 B. 25 C. 9 D. 7

25. If you do a fundraiser for charities in your area and raise $500 total, how much would you give to each charity if you were donating equal amounts to 3 of them? 25.____
    A. $250.00 B. $167.77 C. $50.00 D. $111.11

KEY (CORRECT ANSWERS)

1.	D		11.	C
2.	B		12.	B
3.	A		13.	C
4.	C		14.	A
5.	D		15.	C
6.	B		16.	C
7.	D		17.	B
8.	A		18.	B
9.	A		19.	C
10.	D		20.	B

21. C
22. B
23. C
24. A
25. B

TEST 3

DIRECTIONS: Each question or incomplete statement is followed by several suggested answers or completions. Select the one that BEST answers the question or completes the statement. *PRINT THE LETTER OF THE CORRECT ANSWER IN THE SPACE AT THE RIGHT.*

Questions 1-3.

DIRECTIONS: In answering Questions 1 through 3, choose the correctly spelled word.

1. A. allusion B. alusion C. allusien D. allution 1.____

2. A. altitude B. alltitude C. atlitude D. altlitude 2.____

3. A. althogh B. allthough C. althrough D. although 3.____

Questions 4-9.

DIRECTIONS: In answering Questions 4 through 9, choose the answer that BEST completes the analogy.

4. Odometer is to mileage as compass is to 4.____
   A. speed B. needle C. hiking D. direction

5. Marathon is to race as hibernation is to 5.____
   A. winter B. dream C. sleep D. bear

6. Cup is to coffee as bowl is to 6.____
   A. dish B. spoon C. food D. soup

7. Flow is to river as stagnant is to 7.____
   A. pool B. rain C. stream D. canal

8. Paw is to cat as hoof is to 8.____
   A. lamb B. horse C. lion D. elephant

9. Architect is to building as sculptor is to 9.____
   A. museum B. chisel C. stone D. statue

Questions 10-14.

DIRECTIONS: Questions 10 through 14 are to be answered on the basis of the following graph.

Population of Carroll City Broken Down by Age and Gender (in Thousands)			
Age	Female	Male	Total
Under 15	60	60	120
15-23		22	
24-33		20	44
34-43	13	18	31
44-53	20		67
64 and Over	65	65	130
TOTAL	230	232	462

10. How many people in the city are between the ages of 15-23?
    A. 70   B. 46,000   C. 70,000   D. 225,000

11. Approximately what percentage of the total population of the city was female aged 24-33?
    A. 10%   B. 5%   C. 15%   D. 25%

12. If 33% of the males have a job and 55% of females don't have a job, which of the following statements is TRUE?
    A. Males have approximately 2,600 more jobs than females.
    B. Females have approximately 49,000 more jobs than males.
    C. Females have approximately 26,000 more jobs than males.
    D. None of the above statements are true.

13. How many females between the ages of 15-23 live in Carroll City?
    A. 67,000   B. 24,000   C. 48,000   D. 91,000

14. Assume all males 44-53 living in Carroll City are employed. If two-thirds of males age 44-53 work jobs outside of Carroll City, how many work within city limits?
    A. 31,333
    B. 15,667
    C. 47,000
    D. Cannot answer the question with the information provided

Questions 15-16.

DIRECTIONS: Questions 15 and 16 are labeled as shown. Alphabetize them for filing. Choose the answer that correctly shows the order.

15. (1) AED
    (2) OOS
    (3) FOA
    (4) DOM
    (5) COB

    A. 2-5-4-3-2   B. 1-4-5-2-3   C. 1-5-4-2-3   D. 1-5-4-3-2

15.____

16. Alphabetize the names of the people. Last names are given last.
    (1) Lindsey Jamestown
    (2) Jane Alberta
    (3) Ally Jamestown
    (4) Allison Johnston
    (5) Lyle Moreno

    A. 2-1-3-4-5   B. 3-4-2-1-5   C. 2-3-1-4-5   D. 4-3-2-1-5

16.____

17. Which of the following words is misspelled?
    A. disgust   B. whisper
    C. locale   D. none of the above

17.____

Questions 18-21.

DIRECTIONS: Questions 18 through 21 are to be answered on the basis of the following list of employees.

    Robertson, Aaron
    Bacon, Gina
    Jerimiah, Trace
    Gillette, Stanley
    Jacks, Sharon

18. Which employee name would come in third in alphabetized list?
    A. Robertson, Aaron   B. Jerimiah, Trace
    C. Gillette, Stanley   D. Jacks, Sharon

18.____

19. Which employee's first name starts with the letter in the alphabet that is five letters after the first letter of their last name?
    A. Jerimiah, Trace   B. Bacon, Gina
    C. Jacks, Sharon   D. Gillette, Stanley

19.____

20. How many employees have last names that are exactly five letters long?
    A. 1   B. 2   C. 3   D. 4

20.____

21. How many of the employees have either a first or last name that starts with the letter "G"?   21._____
    A. 1   B. 2   C. 4   D. 5

Questions 22-25.

DIRECTIONS: Questions 22 through 25 are to be answered on the basis of the following chart.

Bicycle Sales (Model #34JA32)							
Country	May	June	July	August	September	October	Total
Germany	34	47	45	54	56	60	296
Britain	40	44	36	47	47	46	260
Ireland	37	32	32	32	34	33	200
Portugal	14	14	14	16	17	14	89
Italy	29	29	28	31	29	31	177
Belgium	22	24	24	26	25	23	144
Total	176	198	179	206	208	207	1166

22. What percentage of the overall total was sold to the German importer?   22._____
    A. 25.3%   B. 22%   C. 24.1%   D. 23%

23. What percentage of the overall total was sold in September?   23._____
    A. 24.1%   B. 25.6%   C. 17.9%   D. 24.6%

24. What is the average number of units per month imported into Belgium over the first four months shown?   24._____
    A. 26   B. 20   C. 24   D. 31

25. If you look at the three smallest importers, what is their total import percentage?   25._____
    A. 35.1%   B. 37.1%   C. 40%   D. 28%

KEY (CORRECT ANSWERS)

1.	A	11.	B
2.	A	12.	C
3.	D	13.	C
4.	D	14.	B
5.	C	15.	D
6.	D	16.	C
7.	A	17.	D
8.	B	18.	D
9.	D	19.	B
10.	C	20.	B

21.	B
22.	A
23.	C
24.	C
25.	A

TEST 4

DIRECTIONS: Each question or incomplete statement is followed by several suggested answers or completions. Select the one that BEST answers the question or completes the statement. *PRINT THE LETTER OF THE CORRECT ANSWER IN THE SPACE AT THE RIGHT.*

Questions 1-6.

DIRECTIONS: In answering Questions 1 through 6, choose the sentence that represents the BEST example of English grammar.

1. A. Joey and me want to go on a vacation next week.
    B. Gary told Jim he would need to take some time off.
    C. If turning six years old, Jim's uncle would teach Spanish to him.
    D. Fax a copy of your resume to Ms. Perez and me.

    1.____

2. A. Jerry stood in line for almost two hours.
    B. The reaction to my engagement was less exciting than I thought it would be.
    C. Carlos and me have done great work on this project.
    D. Two parts of the speech needs to be revised before tomorrow.

    2.____

3. A. Arriving home, the alarm was tripped.
    B. Jonny is regarded as a stand up guy, a responsible parent, and he doesn't give up until a task is finished.
    C. Each employee must submit a drug test each month.
    D. One of the documents was incinerated in the explosion.

    3.____

4. A. As soon as my parents get home, I told them I finished all of my chores.
    B. I asked my teacher to send me my missing work, check my absences, and how did I do on my test.
    C. Matt attempted to keep it concealed from Jenny and me.
    D. If Mary or him cannot get work done on time, I will have to split them up.

    4.____

5. A. Driving to work, the traffic report warned him of an accident on Highway 47.
    B. Jimmy has performed well this season.
    C. Since finishing her degree, several job offers have been given to Cam.
    D. Our boss is creating unstable conditions for we employees.

    5.____

6. A. The thief was described as a tall man with a wiry mustache weighing approximately 150 pounds.
    B. She gave Patrick and I some more time to finish our work.
    C. One of the books that he ordered was damaged in shipping.
    D. While talking on the rotary phone, the car Jim was driving skidded off the road.

    6.____

Questions 7-9.

DIRECTIONS: Questions 7 through 9 are to be answered on the basis of the following graph.

Ice Lake Frozen Flight (2002-2013)		
Year	Number of Participants	Temperature (Fahrenheit)
2002	22	4°
2003	50	33°
2004	69	18°
2005	104	22°
2006	108	24°
2007	288	33°
2008	173	9°
2009	598	39°
2010	698	26°
2011	696	30°
2012	777	28°
2013	578	32°

7. Which two year span had the LARGEST difference between temperatures?
   A. 2002 and 2003
   B. 2011 and 2012
   C. 2008 and 2009
   D. 2003 and 2004

8. How many total people participated in the years after the temperature reached at least 29°?
   A. 2,295
   B. 1,717
   C. 2,210
   D. 4,543

9. In 2007, the event saw 288 participants, while in 2008 that number dropped to 173. Which of the following reasons BEST explains the drop in participants?
   A. The event had not been going on that long and people didn't know about it.
   B. The lake water wasn't cold enough to have people jump in.
   C. The temperature was too cold for many people who would have normally participated.
   D. None of the above reasons explain the drop in participants.

10. In the following list of numbers, how many times does 4 come just after 2 when 2 comes just after an odd number?
    2365247653898632488572486392424
    A. 2
    B. 3
    C. 4
    D. 5

11. Which choice below lists the letter that is as far after B as S is after N in the alphabet?
    A. G
    B. H
    C. I
    D. J

Questions 12-15.

DIRECTIONS: Questions 12 through 15 are to be answered on the basis of the following directory and list of changes.

Directory		
Name	Emp. Type	Position
Julie Taylor	Warehouse	Packer
James King	Office	Administrative Assistant
John Williams	Office	Salesperson
Ray Moore	Warehouse	Maintenance
Kathleen Byrne	Warehouse	Supervisor
Amy Jones	Office	Salesperson
Paul Jonas	Office	Salesperson
Lisa Wong	Warehouse	Loader
Eugene Lee	Office	Accountant
Bruce Lavine	Office	Manager
Adam Gates	Warehouse	Packer
Will Suter	Warehouse	Packer
Gary Lorper	Office	Accountant
Jon Adams	Office	Salesperson
Susannah Harper	Office	Salesperson

Directory Updates:
- Employee e-mail addresses will adhere to the following guidelines: lastnamefirstname@apexindustries.com (ex. Susannah Harper is harpersusannah@apexindustries.com). Currently, employees in the warehouse share one e-mail, distribution@apexindustries.com.
- The "Loader" position will now be referred to as "Specialist I"
- Adam Gates has accepted a Supervisor position within the Warehouse and is no longer a Packer. All warehouse employees report to the two Supervisors and all office employees report to the Manager.

12. Amy Jones tried to send an e-mail to Adam Gates, but it wouldn't send. Which of the following offers the BEST explanation? 12.____
    A. Amy put Adam's first name first and then his last name.
    B. Adam doesn't check his e-mail, so he wouldn't know if he received the e-mail or not.
    C. Adam does not have his own e-mail.
    D. Office employees are not allowed to send e-mails to each other.

13. How many Packers currently work for Apex Industries? 13.____
    A. 2 B. 3 C. 4 D. 5

14. What position does Lisa Wong currently hold? 14.____
    A. Specialist I B. Secretary
    C. Administrative Assistant D. Loader

15. If an employee wanted to contact the office manager, which of the following e-mails should the e-mail be sent to?   15._____
   A. officemanager@apexindustries.com
   B. brucelavine@apexindustries.com
   C. lavinebruce@apexindustries.com
   D. distribution@apexindustries.com

Questions 16-19.

DIRECTIONS: In answering Questions 16 through 19, compare the three names, numbers or addresses.

16. Smiley Yarnell   Smiley Yarnel   Smily Yarnell   16._____
   A. All three are exactly alike.
   B. The first and second are exactly alike.
   C. The second and third are exactly alike.
   D. All three are different.

17. 1583 Theater Drive   1583 Theater Drive   1583 Theatre Drive   17._____
   A. All three are exactly alike.
   B. The first and second are exactly alike.
   C. The second and third are exactly alike.
   D. All three are different.

18. 3341893212   3341893212   3341893212   18._____
   A. All three are exactly alike.
   B. The first and second are exactly alike.
   C. The second and third are exactly alike.
   D. All three are different.

19. Douglass Watkins   Douglas Watkins   Douglass Watkins   19._____
   A. All three are exactly alike.
   B. The first and third are exactly alike.
   C. The second and third are exactly alike.
   D. All three are different.

Questions 20-24.

DIRECTIONS: In answering Questions 20 through 24, you will be presented with a word. Choose the synonym that BEST represents the word in question.

20. Flexible   20._____
   A. delicate   B. inflammable   C. strong   D. pliable

21. Alternative   21._____
   A. choice   B. moderate   C. lazy   D. value

5 (#4)

22. Corroborate   22.____
    A. examine   B. explain   C. verify   D. explain

23. Respiration   23.____
    A. recovery   B. breathing C. sweating D. selfish

24. Negligent   24.____
    A. lazy   B. moderate   C. hopeless D. lax

25. Plumber is to Wrench as Painter is to   25.____
    A. pipe   B. shop   C. hammer   D. brush

KEY (CORRECT ANSWERS)

1. D   11. A
2. A   12. C
3. D   13. A
4. C   14. A
5. B   15. C

6. C   16. D
7. C   17. B
8. B   18. A
9. C   19. B
10. C   20. D

21. A
22. C
23. B
24. D
25. D

CLERICAL ABILITIES TEST
EXAMINATION SECTION
TEST 1

DIRECTIONS: Each question or incomplete statement is followed by several suggested answers or completions. Select the one that BEST answers the question or completes the statement. *PRINT THE LETTER OF THE CORRECT ANSWER IN THE SPACE AT THE RIGHT.*

Questions 1-10.

DIRECTIONS: Questions 1 through 10 consist of lines of names, dates, and numbers. For each question, you are to choose the option (A, B, C, or D) in Column II which EXACTLY matches the information in Column I. *PRINT THE LETTER OF THE CORRECT ANSWER IN THE SPACE AT THE RIGHT.*

SAMPLE QUESTION

Column I
Schneider 11/16/75 581932

Column II
A. Schneider 11/16/75 518932
B. Schneider 11/16/75 581932
C. Schnieder 11/16/75 581932
D. Shnieder 11/16/75 518932

The correct answer is B. Only Option B shows the name, date, and number exactly as they are in Column I. Option A has a mistake in the number. Option C has a mistake in the name. Option D has a mistake in the name and in the number. Now answer Questions 1 through 10 in the same manner.

Column I
1. Johnston 12/26/74 659251

Column II
A. Johnson 12/23/74 659251
B. Johston 12/26/74 659251
C. Johnston 12/26/74 695251
D. Johnston 12/26/74 659251

1.____

2. Allison 1/26/75 9939256

A. Allison 1/26/75 9939256
B. Alisson 1/26/75 9939256
C. Allison 1/26/76 9399256
D. Allison 1/26/75 9993356

2.____

3. Farrell 2/12/75 361251

A. Farell 2/21/75 361251
B. Farrell 2/12/75 361251
C. Farrell 2/21/75 361251
D. Farrell 2/12/75 361151

3.____

4. Guerrero 4/28/72 105689
    A. Guererro 4/28/72 105689
    B. Guererro 4/28/72 105986
    C. Guerrero 4/28/72 105869
    D. Guerrero 4/28/72 105689

4.____

5. McDonnell 6/05/73 478215
    A. McDonnell 6/15/73 478215
    B. McDonnell 6/05/73 478215
    C. McDonnell 6/05/73 472815
    D. MacDonell 6/05/73 478215

5.____

6. Shepard 3/31/71 075421
    A. Sheperd 3/31/71 075421
    B. Shepard 3/13/71 075421
    C. Shepard 3/31/71 075421
    D. Shepard 3/13/71 075241

6.____

7. Russell 4/01/69 031429
    A. Russell 4/01/69 031429
    B. Russell 4/10/69 034129
    C. Russell 4/10/69 031429
    D. Russell 4/01/69 034129

7.____

8. Phillips 10/16/68 961042
    A. Philipps 10/16/68 961042
    B. Phillips 10/16/68 960142
    C. Phillips 10/16/68 961042
    D. Philipps 10/16/68 916042

8.____

9. Campbell 11/21/72 624856
    A. Campbell 11/21/72 624856
    B. Campbell 11/21/72 624586
    C. Campbell 11/21/72 624686
    D. Campbel 11/21/72 624856

9.____

10. Patterson 9/18/71 76199176
    A. Patterson 9/18/72 76191976
    B. Patterson 9/18/71 76199176
    C. Patterson 9/18/72 76199176
    D. Patterson 9/18/71 76919176

10.____

Questions 11-15.

DIRECTIONS: Questions 11 through 15 consist of groups of numbers and letters which you are to compare. For each question, you are to choose the option (A, B, C, or D) in Column I which EXACTLY matches the group of numbers and letters given in Column I.

SAMPLE QUESTION

Column I
B92466

Column II
A. B92644
B. B94266
C. A92466
D. B92466

The correct answer is D. Only Option D in Column II shows the group of numbers and letters EXACTLY as it appears in Column I. Now answer Questions 11 through 15 in the same manner.

	Column I		Column II	
11.	925AC5	A.	952CA5	11.____
		B.	925AC5	
		C.	952AC5	
		D.	925CA6	
12.	Y006925	A.	Y060925	12.____
		B.	Y006295	
		C.	Y006529	
		D.	Y006925	
13.	J236956	A.	J236956	13.____
		B.	J326965	
		C.	J239656	
		D.	J932656	
14.	AB6952	A.	AB6952	14.____
		B.	AB9625	
		C.	AB9652	
		D.	AB6925	
15.	X259361	A.	X529361	15.____
		B.	X259631	
		C.	X523961	
		D.	X259361	

Questions 16-25.

DIRECTIONS: Each of questions 16 through 25 consists of three lines of code letters and three lines of numbers. The numbers on each line should correspond with the code letters on the same line in accordance with the table below.

Code Letter	S	V	W	A	Q	M	X	E	G	K
Corresponding Number	0	1	2	3	4	5	5	7	8	9

On some of the lines, an error exists in the coding. Compare the letters and numbers in each question carefully. If you find an error or errors on:
 only one of the lines in the question, mark your answer A;
 any two lines in the question, mark your answer B;
 all three lines in the question, mark your answer C;
 none of the lines in the question, mark your answer D.

4 (#1)

SAMPLE QUESTION

WQGKSXG   2489068
XEKVQMA   6591453
KMAESXV   9527061

In the above sample, the first line is correct since each code letter listed has the correct corresponding number. On the second line, an error exists because code letter E should have the number 7 instead of the number 5. On the third line, an error exists because the code letter A should have the number 3 instead of the number 2. Since there are errors in two of the three lines, the correct answer is B. Now answer Questions 16 through 25 in the same manner.

16. SWQEKGA   0247983   16._____
    KEAVSXM   9731065
    SSAXGKQ   0036894

17. QAMKMVS   4259510   17._____
    MGGEASX   5897306
    KSWMKWS   9125920

18. WKXQWVE   2964217   18._____
    QKXXQVA   4966413
    AWMXGVS   3253810

19. GMMKASE   8559307   19._____
    AWVSKSW   3210902
    QAVSVGK   4310189

20. XGKQSMK   6894049   20._____
    QSVKEAS   4019730
    GSMXKMV   8057951

21. AEKMWSG   3195208   21._____
    MKQSVQK   5940149
    XGQAEVW   6843712

22. XGMKAVS   6858310   22._____
    SKMAWEQ   0953174
    GVMEQSA   8167403

23. VQSKAVE   1489317   23._____
    WQGKAEM   2489375
    MEGKAWQ   5689324

24. XMQVSKG   6541098   24._____
    QMEKEWS   4579720
    KMEVGKG   9571983

5 (#1)

25. GKVAMEW   88912572   25._____
    AXMVKAE   3651937
    KWAGMAV   9238531

Questions 26-35.

DIRECTIONS: Each of Questions 26 through 35 consists of a column of figures. For each question, add the column of figures and choose the correct answer from the four choices given.

26. 5,665.43   26._____
    2,356.69
    6,447.24
    7,239.65

    A. 20,698.01   B. 21,709.01
    C. 21,718.01   D. 22,609.01

27. 817,209.55   27._____
    264,354.29
     82,368.76
    849,964.89

    A. 1,893.977.49   B. 1,989,988.39
    C. 2,009,077.39   D. 2,013,897.49

28. 156,366.89   28._____
    249,973.23
    823,229.49
     56,869.45

    A. 1,286,439.06   B. 1,287,521.06
    C. 1,297,539.06   D. 1,296,421.06

29. 23,422.15   29._____
    149,696.24
    238,377.53
     86,289.79
    505,533.63

    A. 989,229.34   B. 999,879.34
    C. 1,003,330.34   D. 1,023,329.34

6 (#1)

30.   2,468,926.70
      656,842.28
        49,723.15
      832,369.59

    A. 3,218,062.72   B. 3,808,092.72
    C. 4,007,861.72   D. 4,818,192.72

30.____

31.   524,201.52
    7,775,678.51
    8,345,299.63
  40,628,898.08
  31,374,670.07

    A. 88,646,647.81   B. 88,646,747.91
    C. 88,648,647.91   D. 88,648,747.81

31.____

32.   6,824,829.40
      682,482.94
  5,542,015.27
      775,678.51
  7,732,507.25

    A. 21,557,513.37   B. 21,567,513.37
    C. 22,567,503.37   D. 22,567,513.37

32.____

33.   22,109,405.58
    6,097,093.43
    5,050,073.99
    8,118,050.05
    4,313,980.82

    A. 45,688,593.87   B. 45,688,603.87
    C. 45,689,593.87   D. 45,689,603.87

33.____

34.   79,324,114.19
  99,848,129.74
  43,331,653.31
  41,610,207.14

    A. 264,114,104.38   B. 264,114,114.38
    C. 265,114,114.38   D. 265,214,104.38

34.____

35. 33,729,653.94
      5,959,342.58
     26,052,715.47
      4,452,669.52
      7,079,953.59

   A. 76,374,334.10   B. 76,375,334.10
   C. 77,274,335.10   D. 77,275,335.10

Questions 36-40.

DIRECTIONS: Each of Questions 36 through 40 consists of a single number in Column I and four options in Column II. For each question, you are to choose the option (A, B, C, or D) in Column II which EXACTLY matches the number in Column I.

SAMPLE QUESTION

Column I   Column II
5965121   A. 5956121
                  B. 5965121
                  C. 5966121
                  D. 5965211

The correct answer is B. Only Option B shows the number EXACTLY as it appears in Column I. Now answer Questions 36 through 40 in the same manner.

Column I   Column II
36. 9643242   A. 9643242
                  B. 9462342
                  C. 9642442
                  D. 9463242

37. 3572477   A. 3752477
                  B. 3725477
                  C. 3572477
                  D. 3574277

38. 5276101   A. 5267101
                  B. 5726011
                  C. 5271601
                  D. 5276101

39. 4469329   A. 4496329
                  B. 4469329
                  C. 4496239
                  D. 4469239

40. 2326308   A. 2236308   40.____
                B. 2233608
                C. 2326308
                D. 2323608

KEY (CORRECT ANSWERS)

1.	D	11.	B	21.	A	31.	D
2.	A	12.	D	22.	C	32.	A
3.	B	13.	A	23.	B	33.	B
4.	D	14.	A	24.	D	34.	A
5.	B	15.	D	25.	A	35.	C
6.	C	16.	D	26.	B	36.	A
7.	A	17.	C	27.	D	37.	C
8.	C	18.	A	28.	A	38.	D
9.	A	19.	D	29.	C	39.	B
10.	B	20.	B	30.	C	40.	C

TEST 2

DIRECTIONS: Each question or incomplete statement is followed by several suggested answers or completions. Select the one that BEST answers the question or completes the statement. *PRINT THE LETTER OF THE CORRECT ANSWER IN THE SPACE AT THE RIGHT.*

Questions 1-5.

DIRECTIONS: Each of Questions 1 through 5 consists of a name and a dollar amount. In each question, the name and dollar amount in Column II should be an EXACT copy of the name and dollar amount in Column I. If there is:
- a mistake only in the name, mark your answer A;
- a mistake only in the dollar amount, mark your answer B;
- a mistake in both the name and the dollar amount, mark your answer C;
- no mistake in either the name or the dollar amount, mark your answer D.

SAMPLE QUESTION

Column I
George Peterson
$125.50

Column II
George Petersson
$125.50

Compare the name and dollar amount in Column II with the name and dollar amount in Column I. The name *Petersson* in Column II is spelled *Peterson* in Column I. The amount is the same in both columns. Since there is a mistake only in the name, the answer to the sample question is A. Now answer Questions 1 through 5 in the same manner.

	Column I	Column II	
1.	Susanne Shultz $3440	Susanne Schultz $3440	1._____
2.	Anibal P. Contrucci $2121.61	Anibel P. Contrucci $2112.61	2._____
3.	Eugenio Mendoza $12.45	Eugenio Mendozza $12.45	3._____
4.	Maurice Gluckstadt $4297	Maurice Gluckstadt $4297	4._____
5.	John Pampellonne $4656.94	John Pammpellonne $4566.94	5._____

2 (#2)

Questions 6-11.

DIRECTIONS: Each of Questions 6 through 11 consist of a set of names and addresses, which you are to compare. In each question, the name and addresses in Column II should be an EXACT copy of the name and address in Column I. If there is:
- a mistake only in the name, mark your answer A;
- a mistake only in the address, mark your answer B;
- a mistake in both the name and address, mark your answer C;
- no mistake in either the name or address, mark your answer D.

SAMPLE QUESTION

Column I
Michael Filbert
456 Reade Street
New York, N.Y. 10013

Column II
Michael Filbert
645 Reade Street
New York, N.Y. 10013

Since there is a mistake only in the address (the street number should be 456 instead of 645), the answer to the sample question is B. Now answer Questions 6 through 11 in the same manner.

Column I

6. Hilda Goettelmann
   55 Lenox Rd.
   Brooklyn, N.Y. 11226

7. Arthur Sherman
   2522 Batchelder St.
   Brooklyn, N.Y. 11235

8. Ralph Barnett
   300 West 28 Street
   New York, New York 10001

9. George Goodwin
   135 Palmer Avenue
   Staten Island, New York 10302

10. Alonso Ramirez
    232 West 79 Street
    New York, N.Y. 10024

11. Cynthia Graham
    149-34 83 Street
    Howard Beach, N.Y. 11414

Column II

Hilda Goettelman
55 Lenox Ave.
Brooklyn, N.Y. 11226

Arthur Sharman
2522 Batcheder St.
Brooklyn, N.Y. 11253

Ralph Barnett
300 West 28 Street
New York, New York 10001

George Godwin
135 Palmer Avenue
Staten Island, New York 10302

Alonso Ramirez
223 West 79 Street
New York, N.Y. 10024

Cynthia Graham
149-35 83 Street
Howard Beach, N.Y. 11414

6._____

7._____

8._____

9._____

10._____

11._____

3 (#2)

Questions 12-20.

DIRECTIONS: Questions 12 through 20 are problems in subtraction. For each question do the subtraction and select your answer from the four choices given.

12. 232,921.85
    -179,587.68   12._____

    A. 52,433.17   B. 52,434.17
    C. 53,334.17   D. 53,343,17

13. 5,531,876.29   13._____
    -3,897,158.36

    A. 1,634,717.93   B. 1,644,718.93
    C. 1,734,717.93   D. 1,7234,718.93

14. 1,482,658.22   14._____
    -937,925.76

    A. 544,633.46   B. 544,732.46
    C. 545,632.46   D. 545,732.46

15. 937,828.17   15._____
    -259,673.88

    A. 678,154.29   B. 679,154.29
    C. 688,155.39   D. 699,155.39

16. 760,412.38   16._____
    -263,465.95

    A. 496,046.43   B. 496,946.43
    C. 496,956.43   D. 497,046.43

17. 3,203,902.26   17._____
    -2,933,087.96

    A. 260,814.30   B. 269,824.30
    C. 270,814.30   D. 270,824.30

18. 1,023,468.71   18._____
    -934,678.88

    A. 88,780.83   B. 88,789.83
    C. 88,880.83   D. 88,889.83

19. 831,549.47
    -772,814.78

    A. 58,734.69   B. 58,834.69
    C. 59,735.69   D. 59,834.69

20. 6,306,181.74
    -3,617,376.99

    A. 2,687,904.99   B. 2,688,904.99
    C. 2,689,804.99   D. 2,799,905.99

Questions 21-30.

DIRECTIONS: Each of Questions 21 through 30 consists of three lines of code letters and three lines of numbers. The numbers on each line should correspond with the code letters on the same line in accordance with the table below.

Code Letter	J	U	B	T	Y	D	K	R	L	P
Corresponding Number	0	1	2	3	4	5	5	7	8	9

On some of the lines, an error exists in the coding. Compare the letters and numbers in each question carefully. If you find an error or errors on:
  only *one* of the lines in the question, mark your answer A;
  any *two* lines in the question, mark your answer B;
  all *three* lines in the question, mark your answer C;
  none of the lines in the question, mark your answer D.

SAMPLE QUESTION

BJRPYUR   2079417
DTBPYKJ   5328460
YKLDBLT   4685283

In the above sample, the first line is correct since each code letter listed has the correct corresponding number. On the second line, an error exists because code letter P should have the number 9 instead of the number 8. The third line is correct since each code letter listed has the correct corresponding number. Since there is an error in *one* of the three lines, the correct answer is A. Now answer Questions 21 through 30 in the same manner.

21. BYPDTJL   2495308
    PLRDTJU   9815301
    DTJRYLK   5207486

22. RPBYRJK   7934706
    PKTYLBU   9624821
    KDLPJYR   6489047

23. TPYBUJR   3942107   23.____
    BYRKPTU   2476931
    DUKPYDL   5169458

24. KBYDLPL   6345898   24.____
    BLRKBRU   2876261
    JTULDYB   0318542

25. LDPYDKR   8594567   25.____
    BDKDRJL   2565708
    BDRPLUJ   2679810

26. PLRLBPU   9858291   26.____
    LPYKRDJ   88936750
    TDKPDTR   3569527

27. RKURPBY   7617924   27.____
    RYUKPTJ   7426930
    RTKPTJD   7369305

28. DYKPBJT   5469203   28.____
    KLPJBTL   6890238
    TKPLBJP   3698209

29. BTPRJYL   2397148   29.____
    LDKUTYR   8561347
    YDBLRPJ   4528190

30. ULPBKYT   1892643   30.____
    KPDTRBJ   6953720
    YLKJPTB   4860932

KEY (CORRECT ANSWERS)

1.	A	11.	D	21.	B
2.	C	12.	C	22.	C
3.	A	13.	A	23.	D
4.	D	14.	B	24.	B
5.	C	15.	A	25.	A
6.	C	16.	B	26.	C
7.	C	17.	C	27.	A
8.	D	18.	B	28.	D
9.	A	19.	A	29.	B
10.	B	20.	B	30.	D

CLERICAL ABILITIES
EXAMINATION SECTION
TEST 1

DIRECTIONS: Each question or incomplete statement is followed by several suggested answers or completions. Select the one that BEST answers the question or completes the statement. *PRINT THE LETTER OF THE CORRECT ANSWER IN THE SPACE AT THE RIGHT.*

Questions 1-4.

DIRECTIONS: Questions 1 through 4 are to be answered on the basis of the information given below.

    The most commonly used filing system and the one that is easiest to learn is alphabetical filing. This involves putting records in an A to Z order, according to the letters of the alphabet. The name of a person is filed by using the following order: first, the surname or last name; second, the first name; third, the middle name or middle initial. For example, *Henry C. Young* is filed under *Y* and thereafter under *Young, Henry C.* The name of a company is filed in the same way. For example, *Long Cabinet Co.* is filed under *L* while *John T. Long Cabinet Co.* is filed under *L* and thereafter under *Long, John T. Cabinet Co.*

1. The one of the following which lists the names of persons in the CORRECT alphabetical order is:
   A. Mary Carrie, Helen Carrol, James Carson, John Carter
   B. James Carson, Mary Carrie, John Carter, Helen Carrol
   C. Helen Carrol, James Carson, John Carter, Mary Carrie
   D. John Carter, Helen Carrol, Mary Carrie, James Carson

1._____

2. The one of the following which lists the names of persons in the CORRECT alphabetical order is:
   A. Jones, John C.; Jones, John A.; Jones, John P.; Jones, John K.
   B. Jones, John P.; Jones, John K.; Jones, John C.; Jones, John A.
   C. Jones, John A.; Jones, John C.; Jones, John K.; Jones, John P.
   D. Jones, John K.; Jones, John C.; Jones, John A.; Jones, John P.

2._____

3. The one of the following which lists the names of the companies in the CORRECT alphabetical order is:
   A. Blane Co., Blake Co., Block Co., Blear Co.
   B. Blake Co., Blane Co., Blear Co., Block Co.
   C. Block Co., Blear Co., Blane Co., Blake Co.
   D. Blear Co., Blake Co., Blane Co., Block Co.

3._____

4. You are to return to the file an index card on *Barry C. Wayne Materials and Supplies Co.*
Of the following, the CORRECT alphabetical group that you should return the index card to is
A. A to G   B. H to M   C. N to S   D. T to Z

4.____

Questions 5-10.

DIRECTIONS: In each of Questions 5 through 10, the names of four people are given. For each question, choose as your answer the one of the four names given which should be filed FIRST according to the usual system of alphabetical filing of names, as described in the following paragraph.

In filing names, you must start with the last name. Names are filed in order of the first letter of the last name, then the second letter, etc. Therefore, BAILY would be filed before BROWN, which would be filed before COLT. A name with fewer letters of the same type comes first, i.e., Smith before Smithe. If the last names are the same, the names are filed alphabetically by the first name. If the first name is an initial, a name with an initial would come before a first name that starts with the same letter as the initial. Therefore, I. BROWN would come before IRA BROWN. Finally, if both last name and first name are the same, the name would be filed alphabetically by the middle name, once again an initial coming before a middle name which starts with the same letter as the initial. If there is no middle name at all, the name would come before those with middle initials or names.

SAMPLE QUESTION: A. Lester Daniels
B. William Dancer
C. Nathan Danzig
D. Dan Lester

The last names beginning with D are filed before the last name beginning with L. Since DANIELS, DANCER, and DANZIG all begin with the same three letters, you must look at the fourth letter of the last name to determine which name should be filed first. C comes before I or Z in the alphabet, so DANCER is filed before DANIELS or DANZIG. Therefore, the answer to the above sample question is B.

5. A. Scott Biala
    B. Mary Byala
    C. Martin Baylor
    D. Francis Bauer

5.____

6. A. Howard J. Black
    B. Howard Black
    C. J. Howard Black
    D. John H. Black

6.____

7. A. Theodora Garth Kingston
    B. Theadore Barth Kingston
    C. Thomas Kingston
    D. Thomas T. Kingston

7.____

8. A. Paulette Mary Huerta
    B. Paul M. Huerta
    C. Paulette L. Huerta
    D. Peter A. Huerta

9. A. Martha Hunt Morgan
    B. Martin Hunt Morgan
    C. Mary H. Morgan
    D. Martine H. Morgan

10. A. James T. Meerschaum
    B. James M. Mershum
    C. James F. Mearshaum
    D. James N. Meshum

Questions 11-14.

DIRECTIONS: Questions 11 through 14 are to be answered SOLELY on the basis of the following information.

You are required to file various documents in file drawers which are labeled according to the following pattern:

DOCUMENTS

MEMOS		LETTERS	
File	Subject	File	Subject
84PM1	(A-L)	84PC1	(A-L)
84PM2	(M-Z)	84PC2	(M-Z)

REPORTS		INQUIRIES	
File	Subject	File	Subject
84PR1	(A-L)	84PQ1	(A-L)
84PR2	(M-Z)	84PQ2	(M-Z)

11. A letter dealing with a burglary should be filed in the drawer labeled
    A. 84PM1   B. 84PC1   C. 84PR1   D. 84PQ2

12. A report on Statistics should be found in the drawer labeled
    A. 84PM1   B. 84PC2   C. 84PR2   D. 84PQS

13. An inquiry is received about parade permit procedures. It should be filed in the drawer labeled
    A. 84PM2   B. 84PC1   C. 84PR1   D. 84PQ2

14. A police officer has a question about a robbery report you filed. You should pull this file from the drawer labeled
    A. 84PM1   B. 84PM2   C. 84PR1   D. 84PR2

Questions 15-22.

DIRECTIONS: Each of Questions 15 through 22 consists of four or six numbered names. For each question, choose the option (A, B, C, or D) which indicates the order in which the names should be filed in accordance with the following filing instructions:
- File alphabetically according to last name, then first name, then middle initial.
- File according to each successive letter within a name.
- When comparing two names in which the letters in the longer name are identical to the corresponding letters in the shorter name, the shorter name is filed first.
- When the last names are the same, initials are always filed before names beginning with the same letter.

15. I. Ralph Robinson
    II. Alfred Ross
    III. Luis Robles
    IV. James Roberts

    The CORRECT filing sequence for the above names should be
    A. IV, II, I, III B. I, IV, III, II C. III, IV, I, II D. IV, I, III, II

16. I. Irwin Goodwin
    II. Inez Gonzalez
    III. Irene Goodman
    IV. Ira S. Goodwin
    V. Ruth I. Goldstein
    VI. M.B. Goodman

    The CORRECT filing sequence for the above names should be
    A. V, II, I, IV, III, VI   B. V, II, VI, III, IV, I
    C. V, II, III, VI, IV, I   D. V, II, III, VI, I, IV

17. I. George Allan
    II. Gregory Allen
    III. Gary Allen
    IV. George Allen

    The CORRECT filing sequence for the above names should be
    A. IV, III, I, II B. I, IV, II, III C. III, IV, I, II D. I, III, IV, II

18. A. I, IV, II, III
19. B. I, IV, III, II
20. A. II, V, III, IV, I, VI
21. C. VI, III, II, I, IV, V
22. C. VI, II, III, I, V, IV

Questions 23-30.

DIRECTIONS: The code table below shows 10 letters with matching numbers. For each question, there are three sets of letters. Each set of letters is followed by a set of numbers which may or may not match their correct letter according to the code table. For each question, check all three sets of letters and numbers and mark your answer:
    A. if no pairs are correctly matched
    B. if only one pair is correctly matched
    C. if only two pairs are correctly matched
    D. if all three pairs are correctly matched

CODE TABLE

T	M	V	D	S	P	R	G	B	H
1	2	3	4	5	6	7	8	9	0

SAMPLE QUESTION: TMVDSP – 123456
    RGBHTM – 789011
    DSPRGB – 256789

In the sample question above, the first set of numbers correctly match its set of letters. But the second and third pairs contain mistakes. In the second pair, M is correctly matched with number 1. According to the code table, letter M should be correctly matched with number 2. In the third pair, the letter D is incorrectly matched with number 2. According to the code table, letter D should be correctly matched with number 4. Since only one of the pairs is correctly matched, the answer to this sample question is B.

23.   RSBMRM – 759262
    GDSRVH – 845730
    VDBRTM - 349713

24.   TGVSDR – 183247
    SMHRDP – 520647
    TRMHSR – 172057

25.   DSPRGM – 456782
    MVDBHT – 234902
    HPMDBT - 062491

26.   BVPTRD – 936184
    GDPHMB – 807029
    GMRHMV - 827032

27.   MGVRSH – 283750
    TRDMBS – 174295
    SPRMGV - 567283

28. SGBSDM – 489542 28.____
    MGHPTM – 290612
    MPBMHT - 269301

29. TDPBHM – 146902 29.____
    VPBMRS – 369275
    GDMBHM - 842902

30. MVPTBV – 236194 30.____
    PDRTMB – 47128
    BGTMSM - 981232

KEY (CORRECT ANSWERS)

1.	A	11.	B	21.	C
2.	C	12.	C	22.	B
3.	B	13.	D	23.	B
4.	D	14.	D	24.	B
5.	D	15.	D	25.	C
6.	B	16.	C	26.	A
7.	B	17.	D	27.	D
8.	B	18.	A	28.	A
9.	A	19.	B	29.	D
10.	C	20.	A	30.	A

TEST 2

DIRECTIONS: Each question or incomplete statement is followed by several suggested answers or completions. Select the one that BEST answers the question or completes the statement. *PRINT THE LETTER OF THE CORRECT ANSWER IN THE SPACE AT THE RIGHT.*

Questions 1-10.

DIRECTIONS: Questions 1 through 10 each consists of two columns, each containing four lines of names, numbers and/or addresses. For each question, compare the lines in Column I with the lines in Column II to see if they match exactly, and mark your answer A, B, C, or D, according to the following instructions:
- A. all four lines match exactly
- B. only three lines match exactly
- C. only two lines match exactly
- D. only one line matches exactly

<u>COLUMN I</u>　　　　　　　　　　　　　<u>COLUMN II</u>

1. I. Earl Hodgson　　　　　　　　Earl Hodgson　　　　　　1.____
    II. 1409870　　　　　　　　　　1408970
    III. Shore Ave.　　　　　　　　Schore Ave.
    IV. Macon Rd.　　　　　　　　Macon Rd.

2. I. 9671485　　　　　　　　　　9671485　　　　　　　　2.____
    II. 470 Astor Court　　　　　　470 Astor Court
    III. Halprin, Phillip　　　　　　Halperin, Phillip
    IV. Frank D. Poliseo　　　　　Frank D. Poliseo

3. I. Tandem Associates　　　　Tandom Associates　　　3.____
    II. 144-17 Northern Blvd.　　144-17 Northern Blvd.
    III. Alberta Forchi　　　　　　Albert Forchi
    IV. Kings Park, NY 10751　　Kings Point, NY 10751

4. I. Bertha C. McCormack　　Bertha C. McCormack　　4.____
    II. Clayton, MO　　　　　　　Clayton, MO
    III. 976-4242　　　　　　　　　976-4242
    IV. New City, NY 10951　　　New City, NY 10951

5. I. George C. Morill　　　　　George C. Morrill　　　　5.____
    II. Columbia, SC 29201　　Columbia, SD 29201
    III. Louis Ingham　　　　　　Louis Ingham
    IV. 3406 Forest Ave.　　　　3406 Forest Ave.

6. I. 506 S. Elliott Pl.　　　　　506 S. Elliott Pl.　　　　6.____
    II. Herbert Hall　　　　　　　Hurbert Hall
    III. 4712 Rockaway Pkway　4712 Rockaway Pkway
    IV. 169 E. 7 St.　　　　　　　169 E. 7 St.

2 (#2)

7. I.   345 Park Ave.   345 Park Pl.   7.____
    II. Colman Oven Corp.   Coleman Oven Corp.
    III. Robert Conte   Robert Conti
    IV. 6179846   6179846

8. I.   Grigori Schierber   Grigori Schierber   8.____
    II. Des Moines, Iowa   Des Moines, Iowa
    III. Gouverneur Hospital   Gouverneur Hospital
    IV. 91-35 Cresskill Pl.   91-35 Cresskill Pl.

9. I.   Jeffery Janssen   Jeffrey Janssen   9.____
    II. 8041071   8041071
    III. 40 Rockefeller Plaza   40 Rockafeller Plaza
    IV. 407 6 St.   406 7 St.

10. I.   5971996   5871996   10.____
    II. 3113 Knickerbocker Ave.   31123 Knickerbocker Ave.
    III. 8434 Boston Post Rd.   8424 Boston Post Rd.
    IV. Penn Station   Penn Station

Questions 11-14.

DIRECTIONS: Questions 11 through 14 are to be answered by looking at the four groups of names and addresses listed below (I, II, III, and IV), and then finding out the number of groups that have their corresponding numbered lies exactly the same.

         GROUP I   GROUP II
Line 1. Richmond General Hospital   Richman General Hospital
Line 2. Geriatric Clinic   Geriatric Clinic
Line 3. 3975 Paerdegat St.   3975 Peardegat St.
Line 4. Loudonville, New York 11538   Londonville, New York 11538

         GROUP III   GROUP IV
Line 1. Richmond General Hospital   Richmend General Hospital
Line 2. Geriatric Clinic   Geriatric Clinic
Line 3. 3795 Paerdegat St.   3975 Paerdegat St.
Line 4. Loudonville, New York 11358   Loudonville, New York 11538

1. In how many groups is line one exactly the same?   11.____
       A. Two   B. Three   C. Four   D. None

12. In how many groups is line two exactly the same?   12.____
       A. Two   B. Three   C. Four   D. None

13. In how many groups is line three exactly the same?   13.____
       A. Two   B. Three   C. Four   D. None

3 (#2)

14. In how many groups is line four exactly the same? 14.____
    A. Two   B. Three   C. Four   D. None

Questions 15-18.

DIRECTIONS: Each of Questions 15 through 18 has two lists of names and addresses. Each list contains three sets of names and addresses. Check each of the three sets in the list on the right to see if they are the same as the corresponding set in the list on the left. Mark your answers:
    A. if none of the sets in the right list are the same as those in the left list
    B. if only one of the sets in the right list is the same as those in the left list
    C. if only two of the sets in the right list are the same as those in the left list
    D. if all three sets in the right list are the same as those in the left list

15.   Mary T. Berlinger   Mary T. Berlinger   15.____
      2351 Hampton St.   2351 Hampton St.
      Monsey, N.Y. 20117   Monsey, N.Y. 20117

      Eduardo Benes   Eduardo Benes
      483 Kingston Avenue   473 Kingston Avenue
      Central Islip, N.Y. 11734   Central Islip, N.Y. 11734

      Alan Carrington Fuchs   Alan Carrington Fuchs
      17 Gnarled Hollow Road   17 Gnarled Hollow Road
      Los Angeles, CA 91635   Los Angeles, CA 91685

16.   David John Jacobson   David John Jacobson   16.____
      178 34 St. Apt. 4C   178 53 St. Apt. 4C
      New York, N.Y. 00927   New York, N.Y. 00927

      Ann-Marie Calonella   Ann-Marie Calonella
      7243 South Ridge Blvd.   7243 South Ridge Blvd.
      Bakersfield, CA 96714   Bakersfield, CA 96714

      Pauline M. Thompson   Pauline M. Thomson
      872 Linden Ave.   872 Linden Ave.
      Houston, Texas 70321   Houston, Texas 70321

17.   Chester LeRoy Masterton   Chester LeRoy Masterson   17.____
      152 Lacy Rd.   152 Lacy Rd.
      Kankakee, Ill. 54532   Kankakee, Ill. 54532

      William Maloney   William Maloney
      S. LaCrosse Pla.   S. LaCross Pla.
      Wausau, Wisconsin 52136   Wausau, Wisconsin 52146

      Cynthia V. Barnes   Cynthia V. Barnes
      16 Pines Rd.   16 Pines Rd.
      Greenpoint, Miss. 20376   Greenpoint,, Miss. 20376

18. Marcel Jean Frontenac   Marcel Jean Frontenac   18._____
    8 Burton On The Water   6 Burton On The Water
    Calender, Me. 01471   Calender, Me. 01471

    J. Scott Marsden   J. Scott Marsden
    174 S. Tipton St.   174 Tipton St.
    Cleveland, Ohio   Cleveland, Ohio

    Lawrence T. Haney   Lawrence T. Haney
    171 McDonough St.   171 McDonough St.
    Decatur, Ga. 31304   Decatur, Ga. 31304

Questions 19-26.

DIRECTIONS: Each of Questions 19 through 26 has two lists of numbers. Each list contains three sets of numbers. Check each of the three sets in the list on the right to see if they are the same as the corresponding set in the list on the left. Mark your answers:
- A. if none of the sets in the right list are the same as those in the left list
- B. if only one of the sets in the right list is the same as those in the left list
- C. if only two of the sets in the right list are the same as those in the left list
- D. if all three sets in the right list are the same as those in the left lists

19. 7354183476   7354983476   19._____
    4474747744   4474747774
    5791430231   57914302311

20. 7143592185   7143892185   20._____
    8344517699   8344518699
    9178531263   9178531263

21. 2572114731   257214731   21._____
    8806835476   8806835476
    8255831246   8255831246

22. 331476853821   331476858621   22._____
    6976658532996   6976655832996
    3766042113715   3766042113745

23. 8806663315   88066633115   23._____
    74477138449   74477138449
    211756663666   211756663666

24. 990006966996   99000696996   24.____
     53022219743   53022219843
     4171171117717   4171171177717

25. 24400222433004   24400222433004   25.____
     5300030055000355 5300030055500355
     20000075532002022 20000075532002022

26. 6111666406600011116   61116664066001116   26.____
     7111300117001100733   7111300117001100733
     26666446664476518   26666446664476518

Questions 27-30.

DIRECTIONS: Questions 27 through 30 are to be answered by picking the answer which is in the correct numerical order, from the lowest number to the highest number, in each question.

27. A. 44533, 44518, 44516, 44547   27.____
     B. 44516, 44518, 44533, 44547
     C. 44547, 44533, 44518, 44516
     D. 44518, 44516, 44547, 44533

28. A. 95587, 95593, 95601, 95620   28.____
     B. 95601, 95620, 95587, 95593
     C. 95593, 95587, 95601. 95620
     D. 95620, 95601, 95593, 95587

29. A. 232212, 232208, 232232, 232223   29.____
     B. 232208, 232223, 232212, 232232
     C. 232208, 232212, 232223, 232232
     D. 232223, 232232, 232208, 232208

30. A. 113419, 113521, 113462, 113462   30.____
     B. 113588, 113462, 113521, 113419
     C. 113521, 113588, 113419, 113462
     D. 113419, 113462, 113521, 113588

KEY (CORRECT ANSWERS)

1.	C	11.	A	21.	C
2.	B	12.	C	22.	A
3.	D	13.	A	23.	D
4.	A	14.	A	24.	A
5.	C	15.	C	25.	C
6.	B	16.	B	26.	C
7.	D	17.	B	27.	B
8.	A	18.	B	28.	A
9.	D	19.	B	29.	C
10.	C	20.	B	30.	D

READING COMPREHENSION
UNDERSTANDING AND INTERPRETING WRITTEN MATERIAL
EXAMINATION SECTION
TEST 1

DIRECTIONS: Each question or incomplete statement is followed by several suggested answers or completions. Select the one that BEST answers the question or completes the statement. *PRINT THE LETTER OF THE CORRECT ANSWER IN THE SPACE AT THE RIGHT.*

Questions 1-4.

DIRECTIONS: Questions 1 through 4 are to be answered SOLELY on the basis of the following paragraph.

    An annual leave allowance, which combines leaves previously given for vacation, personal business, family illness, and other reasons shall be granted members. Calculation of credits for such leave shall be on an annual basis beginning January 1st of each year. Annual leave credits shall be based on time served by members during preceding calendar year. However, when credits have been accrued and member retires during current year, additional annual leave credits shall, in this instance, be granted at accrual rate of three days for each completed month of service, excluding terminal leave. If accruals granted for completed months of service extend into following month, member shall be granted an additional three days accrual for completed month. This shall be the only condition where accruals in a current year are granted for vacation period in such year.

1. According to the above paragraph, if a fireman's wife were to become seriously ill so that he would take time off from work to be with her, such time off would be deducted from his _____ leave allowance.   1._____
   A. annual
   B. vacation
   C. personal business
   D. family illness

2. Terminal leave means leave taken   2._____
   A. at the end of the calendar year
   B. at the end of the vacation year
   C. immediately before retirement
   D. before actually earned, because of an emergency

3. A fireman appointed on July 1, 2017 will be able to take his first full or normal annual leave during the period   3._____
   A. July 1, 2017 to June 30, 2018
   B. Jan. 1, 2018 to Dec. 31, 2018
   C. July 1, 2018 to June 30, 2019
   D. Jan. 1, 2019 to Dec. 31, 2019

4. According to the above paragraph, a member who retires on July 15 of this year will be entitled to receive leave allowance based on this year of _____ days.   4._____
   A. 15   B. 18   C. 22   D. 24

5. Fire alarm boxes are electromechanical devices for transmitting a coded signal. In each box, there is a trainwork of wheels. When the box is operated, a spring-activated code wheel begins to revolve. The code number of the box is etched on the circumference of the code wheel, and the latter is associated with the circuit in such a way that when it revolves it causes the circuit to open and close in a predetermined manner, thereby transmitting its particular signal to the central station. A fire alarm box is nothing more than a device for interrupting the flow of current in a circuit in such a way as to produce a coded signal that may be decoded by the dispatchers in the central office.
Based on the above, select the FALSE statement.
   A. Each standard fire alarm box has its own code wheel.
   B. The code wheel operates when the box is pulled.
   C. The code wheel is operated electrically.
   D. Only the break in the circuit by the notched wheel causes the alarm signal to be transmitted to the central office.

5._____

Questions 6-9.

DIRECTIONS: Questions 6 through 9 are to be answered SOLELY on the basis of the following paragraph.

Ventilation, as used in firefighting operations, means opening up a building or structure in which a fire is burning to release the accumulated heat, smoke, and gases. Lack of knowledge of the principles of ventilation on the part of firemen may result in unnecessary punishment due to ventilation being neglected or improperly handled. While ventilation itself extinguishes no fires, when used in an intelligent manner, it allows firemen to get at the fire more quickly, easily, and with less danger and hardship.

6. According to the above paragraph, the MOST important result of failure to apply the principles of ventilation at a fire may be
   A. loss of public confidence   B. waste of water
   C. excessive use of equipment   D. injury to firemen

6._____

7. It may be inferred from the above paragraph that the CHIEF advantage of ventilation is that it
   A. eliminates the need for gas masks
   B. reduces smoke damage
   C. permits firemen to work closer to the fire
   D. cools the fire

7._____

8. Knowledge of the principles of ventilation, as defined in the above paragraph, would be LEAST important in a fire in a
   A. tenement house   B. grocery store
   C. ship's hold   D. lumberyard

8._____

9. We may conclude from the above paragraph that for the well-trained and equipped fireman, ventilation is
   A. a simple matter   B. rarely necessary
   C. relatively unimportant   D. a basic tool

9._____

Questions 10-13.

DIRECTIONS: Questions 10 through 13 are to be answered SOLELY on the basis of the following passage.

    Fire exit drills should be established and held periodically to effectively train personnel to leave their working area promptly upon proper signal and to evacuate the building, speedily but without confusion. All fire exit drills should be carefully planned and carried out in a serious manner under rigid discipline so as to provide positive protection in the event of a real emergency. As a general rule, the local fire department should be furnished advance information regarding the exact date and time the exit drill is scheduled. When it is impossible to hold regular drills, written instructions should be distributed to all employees.
    Depending upon individual circumstances, fires in warehouses vary from those of fast development that are almost instantly beyond any possibility of employee control to others of relatively slow development where a small readily attackable flame may be present for periods of time up to 15 minutes or more during which simple attack with fire extinguishers or small building hoses may prevent the fire development. In any case, it is characteristic of many warehouse fires that at a certain point in development they flash up to the top of the stack, increase heat quickly, and spread rapidly. There is a degree of inherent danger in attacking warehouse type fires, and all employees should be thoroughly trained in the use of the types of extinguishers or small hoses in the buildings and well instructed in the necessity of always staying between the fire and a direct pass to an exit.

10. Employees should be instructed that, when fighting a fire, they MUST
    A. try to control the blaze
    B. extinguish any fire in 15 minutes
    C. remain between the fire and a direct passage to the exit
    D. keep the fire between themselves and the fire exit

11. Whenever conditions are such that regular fire drills cannot be held, then which one of the following actions should be taken?
    A. The local fire department should be notified.
    B. Rigid discipline should be maintained during work hours.
    C. Personnel should be instructed to leave their working area by whatever means are available.
    D. Employees should receive fire drill procedures in writing.

12. The above passage indicates that the purpose of fire exit drills is to train employees to
    A. control a fire before it becomes uncontrollable
    B. act as firefighters
    C. leave the working area promptly
    D. be serious

13. According to the above passage, fire exit drills will prove to be of UTMOST effectiveness if
    A. employee participation is made voluntary
    B. they take place periodically
    C. the fire department actively participates
    D. they are held without advance planning

13.____

Questions 14-16.

DIRECTIONS: Questions 14 through 16 are to be answered SOLELY on the basis of the following paragraph.

The heat output from unit heaters will depend on how fast and how completely dry hot steam fills the unit core. For complete and fast air removal and rapid drainage of condensate, use a trap actuated by water or vapor (inverted bucket trap) and not a trap operated by temperature only (thermostatic or bellows trap). A temperature-actuated trap will hold back the hot condensate until it cools to a point where the thermal element opens. When this happens, the condensate backs up in the heater and reduces the heat output. With a water-actuated trap, this will not happen as the water or condensate is discharged as fast as it is formed.

14. On the basis of the information given in the above paragraph, it can be concluded that the PROPER type of trap to use for a unit heater is a(n) _____ trap.
    A. thermostatic
    B. bellows-type
    C. inverted bucket
    D. temperature

14.____

15. According to the above paragraph, the MAIN reason for using the type of trap specified for a unit heater is to
    A. bring the condensate up to steam temperature
    B. prevent reduction in the heat output of the unit heater
    C. permit cycling of the heater
    D. maintain constant temperature of condensate in the trap

15.____

16. As used in the above paragraph, the word *actuated* means MOST NEARLY
    A. clogged   B. operated   C. cleaned   D. vented

16.____

Questions 17-25.

DIRECTIONS: Questions 17 through 25 are to be answered SOLELY on the basis of the following passage. Each question consists of a statement. You are to indicate whether the statement is TRUE (T) or FALSE (F).

MOVING AN OFFICE

An office with all its equipment is sometimes moved during working hours. This is a difficult task and must be done in an orderly manner to avoid confusion. The operation should be planned in such a way as not to interrupt the progress of work usually done in the office and to make possible the accurate placement of the furniture and records in the new location. If the office moves to a place inside the same building, the desks and files are moved with all their contents. If the movement is to another building, the contents of each desk and file are placed in boxes. Each box is marked with a letter showing the particular section in the new quarters to which it is to be moved. Also marked on each box is the number of the desk or file on which the box is to be placed. Each piece of equipment must have a numbered tag. The number of each piece of equipment is put in soft chalk on the floor in the new office to show the proper location, and several floor plans are made to show where each piece of equipment goes. When the moving is done, someone is stationed at each of the several exits of the old office to see that each box or piece of equipment has its destination clearly marked on it. At the new office, someone stands at each of the several entrances with a copy of the floor plan and directs the placing of the furniture and equipment according to the floor plan. No one should interfere at this point with the arrangements shown on the plan. Improvements in arrangement can be considered and made at a later date.

17. It is a hard job to move an office from one place to another during working hours.   17.____

18. Confusion cannot be avoided if an office is moved during working hours.   18.____

19. The work usually done in an office must be stopped for the day when the office is moved during working hours.   19.____

20. If an office is moved from one floor to another in the same building, the contents of a desk are taken out and put into boxes for moving.   20.____

21. If boxes are used to hold material from desks when moving an office, the box is numbered the same as the desk on which it is to be put.   21.____

22. Letters are marked in soft chalk on the floor at the new quarters to show where the desks should go when moved.   22.____

23. When the moving begins, a person is put at each exit of the old office to check that each box and piece of equipment has clearly marked on it where to go.   23.____

24. A person stationed at each entrance of the new quarters to direct the placing of the furniture and equipment has a copy of the floor plan of the new quarters.   24.____

25. If, while the furniture is being moved into the new office, a person helping at a doorway gets an idea of a better way to arrange the furniture, he should change the planned arrangement and make a record of the change.   25.____

KEY (CORRECT ANSWERS)

1.	A		11.	D
2.	C		12.	C
3.	D		13.	B
4.	B		14.	C
5.	C		15.	B
6.	D		16.	B
7.	C		17.	T
8.	D		18.	F
9.	D		19.	F
10.	C		20.	F

21. T
22. F
23. T
24. T
25. F

TEST 2

DIRECTIONS: Each question or incomplete statement is followed by several suggested answers or completions. Select the one that BEST answers the question or completes the statement. *PRINT THE LETTER OF THE CORRECT ANSWER IN THE SPACE AT THE RIGHT.*

Questions 1-4.

DIRECTIONS: Questions 1 through 4 are to be answered SOLELY on the basis of the following paragraph.

In all cases of homicide, members of the Police Department who investigate will make every effort to obtain statements from dying persons. Such statements are of the greatest importance to the District Attorney. In many cases, there may be a failure to solve the crime if they are not taken. The principal element to be considered in taking the declaration of a dying person is his mental attitude. In order to be admissible in evidence, the person must have no hope of recovery. The patient will be fully interrogated on that point before a statement is taken.

1. In cases of homicide, according to the above paragraph, members of the police force will
    A. try to change the mental attitude of the dying person
    B. attempt to obtain a statement from the dying person
    C. not give the information they obtain directly to the District Attorney
    D. be careful not to injure the dying person unnecessarily

1.____

2. The mental attitude of the person making the dying statement is of GREAT importance because it can determine, according to the above paragraph, whether the
    A. victim should be interrogated in the presence of witnesses
    B. victim will be willing to make a statement of any kind
    C. statement will tell the District Attorney who committed the crime
    D. the statement can be used as evidence

2.____

3. District Attorneys find that statements of a dying person are important, according to the above paragraph, because
    A. it may be that the victim will recover and then refuse to testify
    B. they are important elements in determining the mental attitude of the victim
    C. they present a point of view
    D. it may be impossible to punish the criminal without such a statement

3.____

4. A well-known gangster is found dying from a bullet wound. The patrolman first on the scene, in the presence of witnesses, tells the man that he is going to die and asks, *Who shot you?* The gangster says, *Jones shot me, but he hasn't killed me. I'll live to get him.* He then falls back dead.
According to the above paragraph, this statement is
    A. *admissible* in evidence; the man was obviously speaking the truth
    B. *not admissible* in evidence; the man obviously did not believe that he was dying

4.____

123

C. *admissible* in evidence; there were witnesses to the statement
D. *not admissible* in evidence; the victim did not sign any statement and the evidence is merely hearsay

Questions 5-7.

DIRECTIONS: Questions 5 through 7 are to be answered SOLELY on the basis of the following paragraph.

The factors contributing to crime and delinquency are varied and complex. The home and its immediate environment have been found to be crucial in determining the behavior patterns of the individual, and criminality can frequently be traced to faulty family relationships and a bad neighborhood. But in the search for a clearer understanding of the underlying causes of delinquent and criminal behavior, the total environment must be taken into consideration.

5. According to the above paragraph, family relationships 5.____
   A. tend to become faulty in bad neighborhoods
   B. are important in determining the actions of honest people as well as criminals
   C. are the only important element in the understanding of causes of delinquency
   D. are determined by the total environment

6. According to the above paragraph, the causes of crime and delinquency are 6.____
   A. not simple   B. not meaningless
   C. meaningless   D. simple

7. According to the above paragraph, faulty family relationships FREQUENTLY are 7.____
   A. responsible for varied and complex results
   B. caused when one or both parents have a criminal behavior pattern
   C. independent of the total environment
   D. the cause of criminal acts

Questions 8-10.

DIRECTIONS: Questions 8 through 10 are to be answered SOLELY on the basis of the following paragraph.

A change in the specific problems which confront the police and in the methods for dealing with them has taken place in the last few decades. The automobile is a two-way symbol of this change in policing. It menaces every city with a complicated traffic problem and has speeded up the process of committing a crime and making a getaway, but at the same time has increased the effectiveness of police operations. However, the major concern of police departments continues to be the antisocial or criminal actions and behavior of human beings.

8. On the basis of the above paragraph, it can be stated that, for the most part, in the past few decades the specific problems of a police force
   A. have changed but the general problems have not
   B. as well as the general problems have changed
   C. have remained the same but the general problems have changed
   D. as well as the general problems have remained the same

   8.____

9. According to the above paragraph, advances in science and industry have, in general, made the police
   A. operations less effective from the overall point of view
   B. operations more effective from the overall point of view
   C. abandon older methods of solving police problems
   D. concern themselves more with the antisocial acts of human beings

   9.____

10. The automobile is a *two-way symbol*, according to the above paragraph, because its use
    A. has speeded up getting to and away from the scene of a crime
    B. both helps and hurts police operations
    C. introduces a new antisocial act—traffic violation—and does away with criminals like horse thieves
    D. both increases and decreases speed by introducing traffic problems

    10.____

Questions 11-14.

DIRECTIONS: Questions 11 through 14 are to be answered SOLELY on the basis of the following passage on INSTRUCTIONS TO COIN AND TOKEN CASHIERS.

INSTRUCTIONS TO COIN AND TOKEN CASHIERS

Cashiers should reset the machine registers to an even starting number before commencing the day's work. Money bags received directly from collecting agents shall be counted and receipted for on the collecting agent's form. Each cashier shall be responsible for all coin or token bags accepted by him. He must examine all bags to be used for bank deposits for cuts and holes before placing them in use. Care must be exercised so that bags are not cut in opening them. Each bag must be opened separately and verified before another bag is opened. The machine register must be cleared before starting the count of another bag. The amount shown on the machine register must be compared with the amount on the bag tag. The empty bag must be kept on the table for re-examination should there be a difference between the amount on the bag tag and the amount on the machine register.

11. A cashier should BEGIN his day's assignment by
    A. counting and accepting all money bags
    B. resetting the counting machine register
    C. examining all bags for cuts and holes
    D. verifying the contents of all money bags

    11.____

12. In verifying the amount of money in the bags received from the collecting agent, it is BEST to
    A. check the amount in one bag at a time
    B. base the total on the amount on the collecting agent's form
    C. repeat the total shown on the bag tag
    D. refer to the bank deposit receipt

12.____

13. A cashier is instructed to keep each empty coin bag on his table while verifying its contents CHIEFLY because, as long as the bag is on the table
    A. it cannot be misplaced
    B. the supervisor can see how quickly the cashier works
    C. cuts and holes are easily noticed
    D. a recheck is possible in case the machine count disagrees with the bag tag total

13.____

14. The INSTRUCTIONS indicate that it is NOT proper procedure for a cashier to
    A. assume that coin bags are free of cuts and holes
    B. compare the machine register total with the total shown on the bag tag
    C. sign a form when he receives coin bags
    D. reset the machine register before starting the day's counting

14.____

Questions 15-17.

DIRECTIONS: Questions 15 through 17 are to be answered SOLELY on the basis of the following passage.

The mass media are an integral part of the daily life of virtually every American. Among these media the youngest, television, is the most pervasive. Ninety-five percent of American homes have at least one T.V. set, and on the average that set is in use for about 40 hours each week. The central place of television in American life makes this medium the focal point of a growing national concern over the effects of media portrayals of violence on the values, attitudes, and behavior of an ever-increasing audience.

In our concern about violence and its causes, it is easy to make television a scapegoat. But we emphasize the fact that there is no simple answer to the problem of violence—no single explanation of its causes, and no single prescription for its control. It should be remembered that America also experienced high levels of crime and violence in periods before the advent of television.

The problem of balance, taste and artistic merit in entertaining programs on television are complex. We cannot <u>countenance</u> government censorship of television. Nor would we seek to impose arbitrary limitations on programming which might jeopardize television's ability to deal in dramatic presentations with controversial social issues. Nonetheless, we are deeply troubled by television's constant portrayal of violence, not in any genuine attempt to focus artistic expression on the human condition, but rather in pandering to a public preoccupation with violence that television itself has helped to generate,

15. According to the above passage, television uses violence MAINLY
    A. to highlight the reality of everyday existence
    B. to satisfy the audience's hunger for destructive action

15.____

C. to shape the values and attitudes of the public
D. when it films documentaries concerning human conflict

16. Which one of the following statements is BEST supported by the above passage? 16.____
    A. Early American history reveals a crime pattern which is not related to television.
    B. Programs should give presentations of social issues and never portray violent acts.
    C. Television has proven that entertainment programs can easily make the balance between taste and artistic merit a simple matter.
    D. Values and behavior should be regulated by governmental censorship.

17. Of the following, which word has the same meaning as *countenance*, as used in the above passage? 17.____
    A. Approve   B. Exhibit   C. Oppose   D. Reject

Questions 18-21.

DIRECTIONS: Questions 18 through 21 are to be answered SOLELY on the basis of the following passage.

Maintenance of leased or licensed areas on public parks or land has always been a problem. A good rule to follow in the administration and maintenance of such areas is to limit the responsibility of any lessee or licensee to the maintenance of the structures and grounds essential to the efficient operation of the concession, not including areas for the general use of the public, such as picnic areas, public comfort stations, etc.; except where such facilities are leased to another public agency or where special conditions make such inclusion practicable, and where a good standard of maintenance can be assured and enforced. If local conditions and requirements are such that public use areas are included, adequate safeguards to the public should be written into contracts and enforced in their administration, to insure that maintenance by the concessionaire shall be equal to the maintenance standards for other park property.

18. According to the above passage, when an area on a public park is leased to a concessionaire, it is usually BEST to 18.____
    A. confine the responsibility of the concessionaire to operation of the facilities and leave the maintenance function to the park agency
    B. exclude areas of general public use from the maintenance obligation of the concessionaire
    C. make the concessionaire responsible for maintenance of the entire area including areas of general public use
    D. provide additional comfort station facilities for the area

19. According to the above passage, a valid reason for giving a concessionaire responsibility for maintenance of a picnic area within his leased area is that 19.____
    A. local conditions and requirements make it practicable
    B. more than half of the picnic area falls within his leased area
    C. the concessionaire has leased picnic facilities to another public agency
    D. the picnic area falls entirely within his leased area

20. According to the above passage, a precaution that should be taken when a concessionaire is made responsible for maintenance of an area of general public use in a park is
    A. making sure that another public agency has not previously been made responsible for this area
    B. providing the concessionaire with up-to-date equipment, if practicable
    C. requiring that the concessionaire take out adequate insurance for the protection of the public
    D. writing safeguards to the public into the contract

20.____

KEY (CORRECT ANSWERS)

1.	B	11.	B
2.	D	12.	A
3.	D	13.	D
4.	B	14.	A
5.	B	15.	B
6.	A	16.	A
7.	D	17.	A
8.	A	18.	B
9.	B	19.	A
10.	B	20.	D

TEST 3

DIRECTIONS: Each question or incomplete statement is followed by several suggested answers or completions. Select the one that BEST answers the question or completes the statement. *PRINT THE LETTER OF THE CORRECT ANSWER IN THE SPACE AT THE RIGHT.*

Questions 1-5.

DIRECTIONS: Questions 1 through 5 are to be answered SOLELY on the basis of the following paragraph.

Physical inspections are an important tool for the examiner because he will have to decide the case in many instances on the basis of the inspection report. Most proceedings in a rent office are commenced by the filing of a written application or complaint by an interested party; that is, either the landlord or the tenant. Such an application or complaint must be filed in duplicate in order that the opposing party may be served with a copy of the application or complaint and thus be given an opportunity to answer and oppose it. Sometimes, a further opportunity is given the applicant to file a written rebuttal or reply to his adversary's answer. Often an examiner can make a determination or decision based on the written application, the answer, and the reply to the answer; and, of course, it would speed up operations if it were always possible to make decisions based on written documents only. Unfortunately, decisions can't always be made that way. There are numerous occasions where disputed issues of fact remain which cannot be resolved on the basis of the written statements of the parties. Typical examples are the following: The tenant claims that the refrigerator or stove or bathroom fixture is not functioning properly and the landlord denies this It is obvious that in such cases an inspection of the accommodations is almost the only means of resolving such disputed issues,

1. According to the above paragraph,
   A. physical inspections are made in all cases
   B. physical inspections are seldom made
   C. it is sometimes possible to determine the facts in a case without a physical inspection
   D. physical inspections are made when it is necessary to verify the examiner's determination

   1.____

2. According to the above paragraph, in MOST cases, proceedings are started by a(n)
   A. inspector discovering a violation
   B. oral complaint by a tenant or landlord
   C. request from another agency, such as the Building Department
   D. written complaint by a tenant or landlord

   2.____

3. According to the above paragraph, when a tenant files an application with the rent office, the landlord is
   A. not told about the proceeding until after the examiner makes his determination
   B. given the duplicate copy of the application

   3.____

C. notified by means of an inspector visiting the premises
D. not told about the proceeding until after the inspector has visited the premises

4. As used in the above paragraph, the word *disputed* means MOST NEARLY
   A. unsettled   B. contested   C. definite   D. difficult

5. As used in the above paragraph, the word *resolved* means MOST NEARLY
   A. settled   B. fixed   C. helped   D. amended

Questions 6-10.

DIRECTIONS: Questions 6 through 10 are to be answered SOLELY on the basis of the following paragraph.

The examiner should order or request an inspection of the housing accommodations. His request for a physical inspection should be in writing, identify the accommodations and the landlord and the tenant, and specify precisely just what the inspector is to look for and report on. Unless this request is specific and lists in detail every item which the examiner wishes to be reported, the examiner will find that the inspection has not served its purpose and that even with the inspector's report, he is still in no position to decide the case due to loose ends which have not been completely tied up. The items that the examiner is interested in should be separately numbered on the inspection request and the same number referred to in the inspector's report. You can see what it would mean if an inspector came back with a report that did not cover everything. It may mean a tremendous waste of time and often require a re-inspection.

6. According to the above paragraph, the inspector makes an inspection on the order of
   A. the landlord
   B. the tenant
   C. the examiner
   D. both the landlord and the tenant

7. According to the above paragraph, the reason for numbering each item that an inspector reports on is so that
   A. the report is neat
   B. the report can be easily read and referred to
   C. none of the examiner's requests for information is missed
   D. the report will be specific

8. The one of the following items that is NOT necessarily included in the request for inspection is
   A. location of dwelling
   B. name of landlord
   C. item to be checked
   D. type of building

9. As used in the above paragraph, the word *precisely* means MOST NEARLY
   A. exactly   B. generally   C. usually   D. strongly

10. As used in the above paragraph, the words *in detail* mean MOST NEARLY
    A. clearly   B. item by item   C. substantially   D. completely

Questions 11-13.

DIRECTIONS: Questions 11 through 13 are to be answered SOLELY on the basis of the following passage.

The agreement under which a tenant rents property from a landlord is known as a lease. Generally speaking, leases are classified as either short-term or long-term in duration. They are further subdivided according to the method used to determine the amount of periodic rent payments. Of the following types of lease in use, the more commonly used ones are the following:
1. The straight or fixed lease is one in which rent may be paid in equal amounts throughout the duration of the lease. These are usually restricted to short-term leasing, or somewhat longer-term if clauses in the lease provide for periodic escalation of payments as the economy shifts.
2. Percentage leasing, used for short-term commercial leasing, provides the landlord with a stipulated percentage of a tenant's gross sales from goods and services sold on the premises, in addition to a fixed amount of rent.
3. The net lease, generally long-term (ten years or more), requires the tenant to pay all operating costs, including real estate taxes and insurance. In a net-net lease, the tenant further agrees to meet mortgage interest and principal payments.
4. An escalated lease, which is a long-term lease, requires rent to be of a stipulated base amount which periodically is subject to escalation in accordance with cost-of-living index scales, or in direct proportion to taxes, insurance, and operating costs.

11. Based on the information given in the passage, which type of lease is MOST likely to be advantageous to a landlord if there is a high rate of inflation?
 _____ lease.
 A. Fixed B. Percentage C. Net D. Escalated

12. On the basis of thee above passage, which types of lease would generally be MOST suitable for a well-established textile company which requires permanent facilities for its large operations?
 _____ lease and _____ lease.
 A. Percentage; escalated
 B. Escalated; net
 C. Straight; net
 D. Straight; percentage

13. According to the above passage, the ONLY type of lease which assures the same amount of rent throughout a specified interval is the _____ lease.
 A. straight B. percentage C. net-net D. escalated

Questions 14-15.

DIRECTIONS: Questions 14 and 15 are to be answered SOLELY on the basis of the following passage.

If you like people, if you seek contact with them rather than hide yourself in a corner, if you study your fellow men sympathetically, if you try consistently to contribute something to their success and happiness, if you are reasonably generous with your thought and your time, if you have a partial reserve with everyone but a seeming reserve with no one, you will get along with your superiors, your subordinates, and the human race.

By the scores of thousands, precepts and platitudes have been written for the guidance of personal conduct. The odd part of it is that, despite all of this labor, most of the frictions in modern society arise from the individual's feeling of inferiority, his false pride, his vanity, his unwillingness to yield space to any other man and his consequent urge to throw his own weight around. Goethe said that the quality which best enables a man to renew his own life, in his relation to others, is his capability of renouncing particular things at the right moment in order warmly to embrace something new in the next.

14. On the basis of the above passage, it may be INFERRED that   14.____
  A. a person should be unwilling to renounce privileges
  B. a person should realize that loss of a desirable job assignment may come at an opportune moment
  C. it is advisable for a person to maintain a considerable amount of reserve in his relationship with unfamiliar people
  D. people should be ready to contribute generously to a worthy charity

15. Of the following, the MOST valid implication made by the above passage is that   15.____
  A. a wealthy person who spends a considerable amount of money entertaining his friends is not really getting along with them
  B. if a person studies his fellow men carefully and impartially, he will tend to have good relationships with them
  C. individuals who maintain seemingly little reserve in their relationships with people have in some measure overcome their own feelings of inferiority
  D. most precepts that have been written for the guidance of personal conduct in relationships with other people are invalid

Questions 16-17.

DIRECTIONS: Questions 16 and 17 are to be answered SOLELY on the basis of the following passage.

When a design for a new bank note of the Federal Government has been prepared by the Bureau of Engraving and Printing and has been approved by the Secretary of the Treasury, the engravers begin the work of cutting the design in steel. No one engraver does all the work. Each man is a specialist. One works only on portraits, another on lettering, another on scroll work, and so on. Each engraver, with a steel tool known as a graver, and aided by a powerful magnifying glass, carefully carves his portion of the design into the steel. He knows that one false cut or a slip of his tool, or one miscalculation of width or depth of line, may destroy the merit of his work. A single mistake means that months or weeks of labor will have been in vain. The bureau is proud of the fact that no counterfeiter ever has duplicated the excellent work of its expert engravers.

16. According to the above passage, each engraver in the Bureau of Engraving and Printing
    A. must be approved by the Secretary of the Treasury before he can begin work on the design for a new bank note
    B. is responsible for engraving a complete design of a new bank note by himself
    C. designs new bank notes and submits them for approval to the Secretary of the Treasury
    D. performs sonly a specific part of the work of engraving a design for a new bank note

17. According to the above passage,
    A. an engraver's tools are not available to a counterfeiter
    B. mistakes made in engraving a design can be corrected immediately with little delay in the work of the Bureau
    C. the skilled work of the engravers has not been successfully reproduced by counterfeiter
    D. careful carving and cutting by the engraver is essential to prevent damage to equipment

Questions 18-21.

DIRECTIONS: Questions 18 through 21 are to be answered SOLELY on the basis of the following passage.

In the late fifties, the average American housewife spent $4.50 per day for a family of four on food and 5.15 hours in food preparation, if all of her food was *home prepared*; she spent $5.80 per day and 3.245 hours if all of her food was purchased *partially prepared*; and $6.70 per day and 1.64 hours if all of her food was purchased *ready-to-serve*.

Americans spent about 20 billion dollars for food products in 1941. They spent nearly 70 billion dollars in 1958. They spent 25 percent of their cash income on food in 1958. For the same kinds and quantities of food that consumers bought in 1941, they would have spent only 16% of their cash income in 1958. It is obvious that our food does cost more. Many factors contribute to this increase besides the additional cost that might be attributed to processing. Consumption of more expensive food items, higher marketing margins, and more food eaten in restaurants are other factors.

The Census of Manufacturers gives some indication of the total bill for processing. The value added by manufacturing of food and kindred products amounted to 3.5 billion of the 20 billion dollars spent for food in 1941. In the year 1958, the comparable figure had climbed to 14 billion dollars.

18. According to the above passage, the cash income of Americans in 1958 was MOST NEARLY _____ billion dollars.
    A. 11.2   B. 17.5   C. 70   D. 280

19. According to the above passage, if Americans bought the same kinds and quantities of food in 1958 as they did in 1941, they would have spent MOST NEARLY _____ billion dollars.
    A. 20   B. 45   C. 74   D. 84

20. According to the above passage, the percent increase in money spent for food in 1958 over 1941, as compared with the percentage increase in money spent for food processing in the same years,
    A. was greater
    B. was less
    C. was the same
    D. cannot be determined from the passage

21. In 1958, an American housewife who bought all of her food ready-to-serve saved time, as compared with the housewife who prepared all of her food at home
    A. 1.6 hours daily
    B. 1.9 hours daily
    C. 3.5 hours daily
    D. an amount of time which cannot be determined from the above passage

Questions 22-25.

DIRECTIONS: Questions 22 through 25 are to be answered SOLELY on the basis of the following passage.

Any member of the retirement system who is in city service, who files a proper application for service credit and agrees to deductions from his compensation at triple his normal rate of contribution, shall be credited with a period of city service previous to the beginning of his present membership in the retirement system. The period of service credited shall be equal to the period throughout which such triple deductions are made, but may not exceed the total of the city service the number rendered between his first day of eligibility for membership in the retirement system and the day he last became a member. After triple contributions for all of the first three years of service credit claimed, the remaining service credit may be purchased by a single payment of the sum of the remaining payments. If the total time purchasable exceeds ten years, triple contributions may be made for one-half of such time, and the remaining time purchased by a single payment of the sum of the remaining payments. Credit for service acquired in the above manner may be used only in determining the amount of any retirement benefit. Eligibility for such benefit will, in all cases, be based upon service rendered after the employee's membership last began, and will be exclusive of service credit purchased as described above.

22. According to the above passage, in order to obtain credit for city service previous to the beginning of an employee's present membership in the retirement system, the employee must
    A. apply for the service credit and consent to additional contributions to the retirement system
    B. apply for the service credit before he renews his membership in the retirement system
    C. have previous city service which does not exceed ten years
    D. make contributions to the retirement system for three years

23. According to the information in the above passage, credit for city service previous to the beginning of an employee's present membership in the retirement system is
    A. credited up to a maximum of ten years
    B. credited to any member of the retirement system
    C. used in determining the amount of the employee's benefits
    D. used in establishing the employee's eligibility to receive benefits

23._____

24. According to the information in the above passage, a member of the retirement system may purchase service credit for
    A. the period of time between his first day of eligibility for membership in the retirement system and the date he applies for the service credit
    B. one-half of the total of his previous city service if the total time exceeds ten years
    C. the period of time throughout which triple deductions are made
    D. the period of city service between his first day of eligibility for membership in the retirement system and the day he last became a member

24._____

25. Suppose that a member of the retirement system has filed an application for service credit for five years of previous city service.
    Based on the information in the above passage, the employee may purchase credit for this previous city service by making
    A. triple contributions for three years
    B. triple contributions for one-half of the time and a single payment of the sum of the remaining payments
    C. triple contributions for three years and a single payment of the sum of the remaining payments
    D. a single payment of the sum of the payments

25._____

KEY (CORRECT ANSWERS)

1.	C		11.	D
2.	D		12.	B
3.	B		13.	A
4.	B		14.	B
5.	A		15.	C
6.	C		16.	D
7.	C		17.	C
8.	D		18.	D
9.	A		19.	B
10.	B		20.	B

21. C
22. A
23. C
24. D
25. C

EXAMINATION SECTION
TEST 1

DIRECTIONS: Each question or incomplete statement is followed by several suggested answers or completions. Select the one that BEST answers the question or completes the statement. *PRINT THE LETTER OF THE CORRECT ANSWER IN THE SPACE AT THE RIGHT.*

1. Which one of the following generalizations is MOST likely to be INACCURATE and lead to judgmental errors in communication?
    A. A supervisor must be able to read with understanding.
    B. Misunderstanding may lead to dislike.
    C. Anyone can listen to another person and understand what he means.
    D. It is usually desirable to let a speaker talk until he is finished.

1.____

2. Assume that, as a supervisor, you have been directed to inform your subordinates about the implementation of a new procedure which will affect their work.
   While communicating this information, you should do all of the following EXCEPT
    A. obtain the approval of your subordinates regarding the new procedure
    B. explain the reason for implementing the new procedure
    C. hold a staff meeting at a time convenient to most of your subordinates
    D. encourage a productive discussion of the new procedure

2.____

3. Assume that you are in charge of a section that handles requests for information on matters received from the public. One day, you observe that a clerk under your supervision is using a method to log-in requests for information that is different from the one specified by you in the past. Upon questioning the clerk, you discover that instructions changing the old procedure were delivered orally by your supervisor on a day on which you were absent from the office.
   Of the following, the MOST appropriate action for you to take is to
    A. tell the clerk to revert to the old procedure at once
    B. ask your supervisor for information about the change
    C. call your staff together and tell them that no existing procedure is to be changed unless you direct that it be done
    D. write a memo to your supervisor suggesting that all future changes in procedure are to be in writing and that they be directed to you

3.____

4. At the first meeting with your staff after appointment as a supervisor, you find considerable indifference and some hostility among the participants.
   Of the following, the MOST appropriate way to handle this situation is to
    A. disregard the attitudes displayed and continue to make your presentation until you have completed it
    B. discontinue your presentation but continue the meeting and attempt to find out the reasons for their attitudes

4.____

C. warm up your audience with some good-natured statements and anecdotes and then proceed with your presentation
D. discontinue the meeting and set up personal interviews with the staff members to try to find out the reason for their attitude

5. In order to start the training of a new employee, it has been a standard practice to have him read a manual of instructions or procedures.
This method is currently being replaced by the _____ method.
   A. audio-visual
   B. conference
   C. lecture
   D. programmed instruction

6. Of the following subjects, the one that can usually be successfully taught by a first-line supervisor who is training his subordinates is:
   A. theory and philosophy of management
   B. human relations
   C. responsibilities of a supervisor
   D. job skills

7. Assume that as supervisor you are training a clerk who is experiencing difficulty learning a new task.
Which of the following would be the LEAST effective approach to take when trying to solve this problem? To
   A. ask questions which will reveal the clerk's understanding of the task
   B. take a different approach in explaining the task
   C. give the clerk an opportunity to ask questions about the task
   D. make sure the clerk knows you are watching his work closely

8. One school of management and supervision involves participation by employees in the setting of group goals and in the sharing of responsibility for the operation of the unit.
If this philosophy were applied to a unit consisting of professional and clerical personnel, one should expect
   A. the professional and clerical personnel to participate with equal effectiveness in operating areas and policy areas
   B. the professional personnel to participate with greater effectiveness than the clerical personnel in policy areas
   C. the clerical personnel to participate with greater effectiveness than the professional personnel in operating areas
   D. greater participation by clerical personnel but with less responsibility for their actions

9. With regard to productivity, high morale among employees generally indicates a
   A. history of high productivity
   B. nearly absolute positive correlation with high productivity
   C. predisposition to be productive under facilitating leadership and circumstances
   D. complacency which has little effect on productivity

10. Assume that you are going to organize the professionals and clerks under your supervision into work groups or team of two or three employees.
Of the following, the step which is LEAST likely to foster the successful development of each group is to
    A. allow friends to work together in the group
    B. provide special help and attention to employees with no friends in their group
    C. frequently switch employees from group to group
    D. rotate jobs within the group in order to strengthen group identification

10.____

11. Following are four statements which might be made by an employee to his supervisor during a performance evaluation interview.
Which of the statements BEST provides a basis for developing a plan to improve the employee's performance?
    A. *I understand that you are dissatisfied with my work and I will try harder in the future.*
    B. *I feel that I've been making too many careless clerical errors recently.*
    C. *I am aware that I will be subject to disciplinary action if my work does not improve within one month.*
    D. *I understand that this interview is simply a requirement of your job and not a personal attack on me.*

11.____

12. Three months ago, Mr. Smith and his supervisor, Mrs. Jones, developed a plan which was intended to correct Mr. Smith's inadequate job performance. Now, during a follow-up interview, Mr. Smith, who thought his performance had satisfactorily improved, has been informed that Mrs. Jones is still dissatisfied with his work.
Of the following, it is MOST likely that the disagreement occurred because, when formulating the plan, they did NOT
    A. set realistic goals for Mr. Smith's performance
    B. set a reasonable time limit for Mr. Smith to effect his improvement in performance
    C. provide for adequate training to improve Mr. Smith's skills
    D. establish performance standards for measuring Mr. Smith's progress

12.____

13. When a supervisor delegates authority to subordinates, there are usually many problems to overcome, such as inadequately trained subordinates and poor planning.
All of the following are means of increasing the effectiveness of delegation EXCEPT:
    A. Defining assignments in the light of results expected
    B. Maintaining open lines of communication
    C. Establishing tight controls so that subordinates will stay within the bounds of the area of delegation
    D. Providing rewards for successful assumption of authority by a subordinate

13.____

14. Assume that one of your subordinates has arrived late for work several times during the current month. The last time he was late you had warned him that another unexcused lateness would result informal disciplinary action.
If the employee arrives late for work again during this month, the FIRST action you should take is to
    A. give the employee a chance to explain this lateness
    B. give the employee a written copy of your warning
    C. tell the employee that you are recommending formal disciplinary action
    D. tell the employee that you will give him only one more chance before recommending formal disciplinary action

15. In trying to decide how many subordinates a manager can control directly, one of the determinants is how much the manager can reduce the frequency and time consumed in contacts with his subordinates.
Of the following, the factor which LEAST influences the number and direction of these contacts is:
    A. How well the manager delegates authority
    B. The rate at which the organization is changing
    C. The control techniques used by the manager
    D. Whether the activity is line or staff

16. Systematic rotation of employees through lateral transfer within a government organization to provide for managerial development is
    A. *good*, because systematic rotation develops specialists who learn to do many jobs well
    B. *bad*, because the outsider upsets the status quo of the existing organization
    C. *good*, because rotation provides challenge and organizational flexibility
    D. *bad*, because it is upsetting to employees to be transferred within a service

17. Assume that you are required to provide an evaluation of the performance of your subordinates.
Of the following factors, it is MOST important that the performance evaluation include a rating of each employee's
    A. initiative   B. productivity   C. intelligence   D. personality

18. When preparing performance evaluations of your subordinates, one way to help assure that you are rating each employee fairly is to
    A. prepare a list of all employees and all the rating factors and rate all employees on one rating factor before going on to the next factor
    B. prepare a list of all your employees and all the rating factors and rate each employee on all factors before going on to the next employee
    C. discuss all the ratings you anticipate giving with another supervisor in order to obtain an unbiased opinion
    D. discuss each employee with his co-workers in order to obtain peer judgment of worth before doing any rating

19. A managerial plan which would include the GREATEST control is a plan which is
    A. spontaneous and geared to each new job that is received
    B. detailed and covering an extended time period
    C. long-range and generalized, allowing for various interpretations
    D. specific and prepared daily

20. Assume that you are preparing a report which includes statistical data covering increases in budget allocations of four agencies for the past ten years.
    For you to represent the statistical data pictorially or graphically within the report is a
    A. *poor* idea, because you should be able to make statistical data understandable through the use of words
    B. *good* idea, because it is easier for the reader to understand pictorial representation rather than quantities of words conveying statistical data
    C. *poor* idea, because using pictorial representation in a report may make the report too expensive to print
    D. *good* idea, because a pictorial representation makes the report appear more attractive than the use of many words to convey the statistical data

KEY (CORRECT ANSWERS)

1.	C	11.	A
2.	A	12.	B
3.	B	13.	C
4.	D	14.	A
5.	D	15.	D
6.	D	16.	C
7.	D	17.	B
8.	B	18.	A
9.	C	19.	B
10.	C	20.	B

TEST 2

DIRECTIONS: Each question or incomplete statement is followed by several suggested answers or completions. Select the one that BEST answers the question or completes the statement. *PRINT THE LETTER OF THE CORRECT ANSWER IN THE SPACE AT THE RIGHT.*

1. Research studies have shown that supervisors of groups with high production records USUALLY
   A. give detailed instructions, constantly check on progress, and insist on approval of all decisions before implementation
   B. do considerable paperwork and other work similar to that performed by subordinates
   C. think of themselves as team members on the same level as others in the work group
   D. perform tasks traditionally associated with managerial functions

1.____

2. Mr. Smith, a bureau chief, is summoned by his agency's head in a conference to discuss Mr. Jones, an accountant who works in one of the divisions of his bureau. Mr. Jones has committed an error of such magnitude as to arouse the agency head's concern.
   After agreeing with the other conferees that a severe reprimand would be the appropriate punishment, Mr. Smith SHOULD
   A. arrange for Mr. Jones to explain the reasons for his error to the agency head
   B. send a memorandum to Mr. Jones, being careful that the language emphasizes the nature of the error rather than Mr. Jones' personal faults
   C. inform Mr. Jones' immediate supervisor of the conclusion reached at the conference, and let the supervisor take the necessary action
   D. suggest to the agency head that no additional action be taken against Mr. Jones because no further damage will be caused by the error

2.____

3. Assume that Ms. Thomson, a unit chief, has determined that the findings of an internal audit have been seriously distorted as a result of careless errors. The audit had been performed by a group of auditors in her unit and the errors were overlooked by the associate accountant in charge of the audit. Ms. Thomson has decided to delay discussing the matter with the associate accountant and the staff who performed the audit until she verifies certain details, which may require prolonged investigation.
   Mrs. Thomson's method of handling this situation is
   A. *appropriate*; employees should not be accused of wrongdoing until all the facts have been determined
   B. *inappropriate*; the employees involved may assume that the errors were considered unimportant
   C. *appropriate*; employees are more likely to change their behavior as a result of disciplinary action taken after a *cooling off* period
   D. *inappropriate*; the employees involved may have forgotten the details and become emotionally upset when confronted with the facts

3.____

4. After studying the financial situation in his agency, an administrative accountant decides to recommend centralization of certain accounting functions which are being performed in three different bureaus of the organization
The one of the following which is MOST likely to be a DISADVANTAE if this recommendation is implemented is that
   A. there may be less coordination of the accounting procedure because central direction is not so close to the day-to-day problems as the personnel handling them in each specialized accounting unit
   B. the higher management levels would not be able to make emergency decisions in as timely a manner as the more involved, lower-level administrators who are closer to the problem
   C. it is more difficult to focus the attention of the top management in order to resolve accounting problems because of the many other activities top management is involved in at the same time
   D. the accuracy of upward and inter-unit communication may be reduced because centralization may require insertion of more levels of administration in the chain of command

4.____

5. Of the following assumptions about the role of conflict in an organization, the one which is the MOST accurate statement of the approach of modern management theorists is that conflict
   A. can usually be avoided or controlled
   B. serves as a vital element in organizational change
   C. works against attainment of organizational goals
   D. provides a constructive outlet for problem employees

5.____

6. Which of the following is generally regarded as the BEST approach for a supervisor to follow in handling grievances brought by subordinates?
   A. Avoid becoming involved personally
   B. Involve the union representative in the first stage of discussion
   C. Settle the grievance as soon as possible
   D. Arrange for arbitration by a third party

6.____

7. Assume that supervisors of similar-sized accounting units in city, state, and federal offices were interviewed and observed at their work. It was found that the ways they acted in and viewed their roles tended to be very similar, regardless of who employed them.
Which of the following is the BEST explanation of this similarity
   A. A supervisor will ordinarily behave in conformance to his own self-image.
   B. Each role in an organization, including the supervisory role, calls for a distinct type of personality.
   C. The supervisor role reflects an exceptionally complex pattern of human response.
   D. The general nature of the duties and responsibilities of the supervisory position determines the role.

7.____

8. Which of the following is NOT consistent with the findings of recent research about the characteristics of successful top managers?
   A. They are *inner-directed* and not overly concerned with pleasing others.
   B. They are challenged by situations filled with high risk and ambiguity.
   C. They tend to stay on the same job for long periods of time.
   D. They consider it more important to handle critical assignments successfully than to do routine work well.

9. As a supervisor, you have to give subordinates operational guidelines. Of the following, the BEST reason for providing them with information about the overall objectives within which their operations fit is that the subordinates will
   A. be more likely to carry out the operation according to your expectations
   B. know that there is a legitimate reason for carrying out the operation in the way you have prescribed
   C. be more likely to handle unanticipated problems that may arise without having to take up your time
   D. more likely to transmit the operating instructions correctly to their subordinates

10. A supervisor holds frequent meetings with his staff. Of the following, the BEST approach he can take in order to elicit productive discussions at these meetings is for him to
    A. ask questions of those who attend
    B. include several levels of supervisors at the meetings
    C. hold the meetings at a specified time each week
    D. begin each meeting with a statement that discussion is welcomed

11. Of the following, the MOST important action that a supervisor can take to increase the productivity of a subordinate is to
    A. increase his uninterrupted work time
    B. increase the number of reproducing machines available in the office
    C. provide clerical assistance whenever he requests it
    D. reduce the number of his assigned tasks

12. Assume that, as a supervisor, you find out that you often must countermand or modify your original staff memos. If this practice continues, which one of the following situations is MOST likely to occur? The
    A. staff will not bother to read your memos
    B. office files will become cluttered
    C. staff will delay acting on your memos
    D. memos will be treated routinely

13. In making management decisions, the committee approach is often used by managers. Of the following, the BEST reason for using this approach is to
    A. prevent any one individual from assuming too much authority
    B. allow the manager to bring a wider range of experience and judgment to bear on the problem

C. allow the participation of all staff members, which will make them feel more committed to the decisions reached
D. permit the rapid transmission of information about decisions reached to the staff members concerned

14. In establishing standards for the measurement of the performance of a management project team, it is MOST important for the project manager to
   A. identify and define the objectives of the project
   B. determine the number of people who will be assigned to the project team
   C. evaluate the skills of the staff who will be assigned to the project team
   D. estimate fairly accurately the length of time required to complete each phase of the project

14.____

15. It is virtually impossible to tell an employee either that he is not good as another employee or that he does not measure up to a desirable level of performance, without having him feel threatened, rejected, and discouraged.
In accordance with the foregoing observation, a supervisor who is concerned about the performance of the less efficient members of his staff should realize that
   A. he might obtain better results by not discussing the quality and quantity of their work with them, but by relying instead on the written evaluation of their performance to motivate their improvement
   B. since he is required to discuss their performance with them, he should do so in words of encouragement and in so friendly a manner as to not destroy their morale
   C. he might discuss their work in a general way, without mentioning any of the specifics about the quality of their performance, with the expectation that they would understand the full implications of his talk
   D. he should make it a point, while telling them of their poor performance, to mention that their work is as good as that of some of the other employees in the unit

15.____

16. Some advocates of management-by-objectives procedures in public agencies have been urging that this method of operations be expanded to encompass all agencies of the government, for one or more of the following reasons, not all of which may be correct:
   I. The MBO method is likely to succeed because it embraces the practice of setting near-term goals for the subordinate manager, reviewing accomplishments at an appropriate time, and repeating this process indefinitely
   II. Provision for authority to perform the tasks assigned as goals in the MBO method is normally not needed because targets are set in quantitative or qualitative terms and specific times for accomplishment are arranged in short-term, repetitive intervals
   III. Many other appraisal-of-performance programs failed because both supervisors and subordinates resisted them, while the MBO approach is not instituted until there is an organizational commitment to it
   IV. Personal accountability is clearly established through the MBO approach because verifiable results are set up in the process of formulating the targets

16.____

Which of the choices below includes ALL of the foregoing statements that are CORRECT?
A. I, III B. II, IV C. I, II, III, IV D. I, III, IV

17. In preparing an organizational structure, the PRINCIPAL guideline for locating staff units is to place them
    A. all under a common supervisor
    B. as close as possible to the activities they serve
    C. as close to the chief executive as possible without over-extending his span of control
    D. at the lowest operational level

18. The relative importance of any unit in a department can be LEAST reliably judged by the
    A. amount of office space allocated to the unit
    B. number of employees in the unit
    C. rank of the individual who heads the unit
    D. rank of the individual to whom the unit head reports directly

19. Those who favor Planning-Programming-Budgeting Systems (PPBS) as a new method of governmental financial administration emphasize that PPBS
    A. applies statistical measurements which correlate highly with criteria
    B. makes possible economic systems analysis, including an explicit examination of alternatives
    C. makes available scarce government resources which can be coordinated on a government-wide basis and shared between local units of government
    D. shifts the emphasis in budgeting methods to an automated system of data processing

20. The term applied to computer processing which processes data concurrently with a given activity and provides results soon enough to influence the selection of a course of action is _____ processing.
    A. realtime   B. batch
    C. random access   D. integrated data

KEY (CORRECT ANSWERS)

1.	D	11.	A
2.	C	12.	C
3.	B	13.	B
4.	D	14.	A
5.	B	15.	B
6.	C	16.	D
7.	D	17.	B
8.	C	18.	B
9.	C	19.	B
10.	A	20.	A

PHILOSOPHY, PRINCIPLES, PRACTICES, AND TECHNICS OF SUPERVISION, ADMINISTRATION, MANAGEMENT, AND ORGANIZATION

TABLE OF CONTENTS

	Page
MEANING OF SUPERVISION	1
THE OLD AND THE NEW SUPERVISION	1
THE EIGHT (8) BASIC PRINCIPLES OF THE NEW SUPERVISION	1
I. Principle of Responsibility	1
II. Principle of Authority	2
III. Principle of Self-Growth	2
IV. Principle of Individual Worth	2
V. Principle of Creative Leadership	2
VI. Principle of Success and Failure	2
VII. Principle of Science	3
VIII. Principle of Cooperation	3
WHAT IS ADMINISTRATION?	3
I. Practices Commonly Classed as "Supervisory"	3
II. Practices Commonly Classed as "Administrative"	3
III. Practices Commonly Classed as Both "Supervisory" and "Administrative"	4
RESPONSIBILITIES OF THE SUPERVISOR	4
COMPETENCIES OF THE SUPERVISOR	4
THE PROFESSIONAL SUPERVISOR-EMPLOYEE RELATIONSHIP	4
MINI-TEXT IN SUPERVISION, ADMINISTRATION, MANAGEMENT, AND ORGANIZATION	5
I. Brief Highlights	5
A. Levels of Management	6
B. What the Supervisor Must Learn	6
C. A Definition of Supervision	6
D. Elements of the Team Concept	6
E. Principles of Organization	6
F. The Four Important Parts of Every Job	7
G. Principles of Delegation	7
H. Principles of Effective Communications	7
I. Principles of Work Improvement	7
J. Areas of Job Improvement	7
K. Seven Key Points in Making Improvements	8

	L.	Corrective Techniques for Job Improvement	8
	M.	A Planning Checklist	8
	N.	Five Characteristics of Good Directions	9
	O.	Types of Directions	9
	P.	Controls	9
	Q.	Orienting the New Employee	9
	R.	Checklist for Orienting New Employees	9
	S.	Principles of Learning	10
	T.	Causes of Poor Performance	10
	U.	Four Major Steps in On-the-Job Instructions	10
	V.	Employees Want Five Things	10
	W.	Some Don'ts in Regard to Praise	11
	X.	How to Gain Your Workers' Confidence	11
	Y.	Sources of Employee Problems	11
	Z.	The Supervisor's Key to Discipline	11
	AA.	Five Important Processes of Management	12
	BB.	When the Supervisor Fails to Plan	12
	CC.	Fourteen General Principles of Management	12
	DD.	Change	12
II.	Brief Topical Summaries		13
	A.	Who/What is the Supervisor?	13
	B.	The Sociology of Work	13
	C.	Principles and Practices of Supervision	14
	D.	Dynamic Leadership	14
	E.	Processes for Solving Problems	15
	F.	Training for Results	15
	G.	Health, Safety, and Accident Prevention	16
	H.	Equal Employment Opportunity	16
	I.	Improving Communications	16
	J.	Self-Development	17
	K.	Teaching and Training	17
		1. The Teaching Process	17
		a. Preparation	17
		b. Presentation	18
		c. Summary	18
		d. Application	18
		e. Evaluation	18
		2. Teaching Methods	18
		a. Lecture	18
		b. Discussion	18
		c. Demonstration	19
		d. Performance	19
		e. Which Method to Use	19

PHILOSOPHY, PRINCIPLES, PRACTICES, AND TECHNICS
OF
SUPERVISION, ADMINISTRATION, MANAGEMENT, AND ORGANIZATION

MEANING OF SUPERVISION

The extension of the democratic philosophy has been accompanied by an extension in the scope of supervision. Modern leaders and supervisors no longer think of supervision in the narrow sense of being confined chiefly to visiting employees, supplying materials, or rating the staff. They regard supervision as being intimately related to all the concerned agencies of society, they speak of the supervisor's function in terms of "growth," rather than the "improvement" of employees.

This modern concept of supervision may be defined as follows: Supervision is leadership and the development of leadership within groups which are cooperatively engaged in inspection, research, training, guidance, and evaluation.

THE OLD AND THE NEW SUPERVISION

TRADITIONAL
1. Inspection
2. Focused on the employee
3. Visitation
4. Random and haphazard
5. Imposed and authoritarian
6. One person usually

MODERN
1. Study and analysis
2. Focused on aims, materials, methods, supervisors, employees, environment
3. Demonstrations, intervisitation, workshops, directed reading, bulletins, etc.
4. Definitely organized and planned (scientific)
5. Cooperative and democratic
6. Many persons involved (creative)

THE EIGHT (8) BASIC PRINCIPLES OF THE NEW SUPERVISION

I. Principle of Responsibility
    Authority to act and responsibility for acting must be joined.
    A. If you give responsibility, give authority.
    B. Define employee duties clearly.
    C. Protect employees from criticism by others.
    D. Recognize the rights as well as obligations of employees.
    E. Achieve the aims of a democratic society insofar as it is possible within the area of your work.
    F. Establish a situation favorable to training and learning.
    G. Accept ultimate responsibility for everything done in your section, unit, office, division, department.
    H. Good administration and good supervision are inseparable.

II. Principle of Authority
The success of the supervisor is measured by the extent to which the power of authority is not used.
- A. Exercise simplicity and informality in supervision
- B. Use the simplest machinery of supervision
- C. If it is good for the organization as a whole, it is probably justified.
- D. Seldom be arbitrary or authoritative.
- E. Do not base your work on the power of position or of personality.
- F. Permit and encourage the free expression of opinions.

III. Principle of Self-Growth
The success of the supervisor is measured by the extent to which, and the speed with which, he is no longer needed.
- A. Base criticism on principles, not on specifics.
- B. Point out higher activities to employees.
- C. Train for self-thinking by employees to meet new situations.
- D. Stimulate initiative, self-reliance, and individual responsibility
- E. Concentrate on stimulating the growth of employees rather than on removing defects.

IV. Principle of Individual Worth
Respect for the individual is a paramount consideration in supervision.
- A. Be human and sympathetic in dealing with employees.
- B. Don't nag about things to be done.
- C. Recognize the individual differences among employees and seek opportunities to permit best expression of each personality.

V. Principle of Creative Leadership
The best supervision is that which is not apparent to the employee.
- A. Stimulate, don't drive employees to creative action.
- B. Emphasize doing good things.
- C. Encourage employees to do what they do best.
- D. Do not be too greatly concerned with details of subject or method.
- E. Do not be concerned exclusively with immediate problems and activities.
- F. Reveal higher activities and make them both desired and maximally possible.
- G. Determine procedures in the light of each situation but see that these are derived from a sound basic philosophy.
- H. Aid, inspire, and lead so as to liberate the creative spirit latent in all good employees.

VI. Principle of Success and Failure
There are no unsuccessful employees, only unsuccessful supervisors who have failed to give proper leadership.
- A. Adapt suggestions to the capacities, attitudes, and prejudices of employees.
- B. Be gradual, be progressive, be persistent.
- C. Help the employee find the general principle; have the employee apply his own problem to the general principle.
- D. Give adequate appreciation for good work and honest effort.
- E. Anticipate employee difficulties and help to prevent them.
- F. Encourage employees to do the desirable things they will do anyway.
- G. Judge your supervision by the results it secures.

VII. Principle of Science
Successful supervision is scientific, objective, and experimental. It is based on facts, not on prejudices.
- A. Be cumulative in results.
- B. Never divorce your suggestions from the goals of training.
- C. Don't be impatient of results.
- D. Keep all matters on a professional, not a personal, level.
- E. Do not be concerned exclusively with immediate problems and activities.
- F. Use objective means of determining achievement and rating where possible.

VIII. Principle of Cooperation
Supervision is a cooperative enterprise between supervisor and employee.
- A. Begin with conditions as they are.
- B. Ask opinions of all involved when formulating policies.
- C. Organization is as good as its weakest link.
- D. Let employees help to determine policies and department programs.
- E. Be approachable and accessible—physically and mentally.
- F. Develop pleasant social relationships.

WHAT IS ADMINISTRATION

Administration is concerned with providing the environment, the material facilities, and the operational procedures that will promote the maximum growth and development of supervisors and employees. (Organization is an aspect and a concomitant of administration.)

There is no sharp line of demarcation between supervision and administration; these functions are intimately interrelated and, often, overlapping. They are complementary activities.

I. Practices Commonly Classed as "Supervisory"
- A. Conducting employees' conferences
- B. Visiting sections, units, offices, divisions, departments
- C. Arranging for demonstrations
- D. Examining plans
- E. Suggesting professional reading
- F. Interpreting bulletins
- G. Recommending in-service training courses
- H. Encouraging experimentation
- I. Appraising employee morale
- J. Providing for intervisitation

II. Practices Commonly Classified as "Administrative"
- A. Management of the office
- B. Arrangement of schedules for extra duties
- C. Assignment of rooms or areas
- D. Distribution of supplies
- E. Keeping records and reports
- F. Care of audio-visual materials
- G. Keeping inventory records
- H. Checking record cards and books

      I.   Programming special activities
      J.   Checking on the attendance and punctuality of employees

III.   Practices Commonly Classified as Both "Supervisory" and "Administrative"
      A.   Program construction
      B.   Testing or evaluating outcomes
      C.   Personnel accounting
      D.   Ordering instructional materials

RESPONSIBILITIES OF THE SUPERVISOR

A person employed in a supervisory capacity must constantly be able to improve his own efficiency and ability. He represent the employer to the employees and only continuous self-examination can make him a capable supervisor.

Leadership and training are the supervisor's responsibility. An efficient working unit is one in which the employees work with the supervisor. It is his job to bring out the best in his employees. He must always be relaxed, courteous, and calm in his association with his employees. Their feelings are important, and a harsh attitude does not develop the most efficient employees.

COMPETENCES OF THE SUPERVISOR

      I.   Complete knowledge of the duties and responsibilities of his position.
      II.   To be able to organize a job, plan ahead, and carry through.
      III.   To have self-confidence and initiative.
      IV.   To be able to handle the unexpected situation and make quick decisions.
      V.   To be able to properly train subordinates in the positions they are best suited for.
      VI.   To be able to keep good human relations among his subordinates.
      VII.   To be able to keep good human relations between his subordinates and himself and to earn their respect and trust.

THE PROFESSIONAL SUPERVISOR-EMPLOYEE RELATIONSHIP

There are two kinds of efficiency: one kind is only apparent and is produced in organizations through the exercise of mere discipline; this is but a simulation of the second, or true, efficiency which springs from spontaneous cooperation. If you are a manager, no matter how great or small your responsibility, it is your job, in the final analysis, to create and develop this involuntary cooperation among the people whom you supervise. For, no matter how powerful a combination of money, machines, and materials a company may have, this is a dead and sterile thing without a team of willing, thinking, and articulate people to guide it.

The following 21 points are presented as indicative of the exemplary basic relationship that should exist between supervisor and employee:

1. Each person wants to be liked and respected by his fellow employee and wants to be treated with consideration and respect by his superior.
2. The most competent employee will make an error. However, in a unit where good relations exist between the supervisor and his employees, tenseness and fear do not exist. Thus, errors are not hidden or covered up, and the efficiency of a unit is not impaired.

3. Subordinates resent rules, regulations, or orders that are unreasonable or unexplained.
4. Subordinates are quick to resent unfairness, harshness, injustices, and favoritism.
5. An employee will accept responsibility if he knows that he will be complimented for a job well done, and not too harshly chastised for failure; that his supervisor will check the cause of the failure, and, if it was the supervisor's fault, he will assume the blame therefore. If it was the employee's fault, his supervisor will explain the correct method or means of handling the responsibility.
6. An employee wants to receive credit for a suggestion he has made, that is used. If a suggestion cannot be used, the employee is entitled to an explanation. The supervisor should not say "no" and close the subject.
7. Fear and worry slow up a worker's ability. Poor working environment can impair his physical and mental health. A good supervisor avoids forceful methods, threats, and arguments to get a job done.
8. A forceful supervisor is able to train his employees individually and as a team, and is able to motivate them in the proper channels.
9. A mature supervisor is able to properly evaluate his subordinates and to keep them happy and satisfied.
10. A sensitive supervisor will never patronize his subordinates.
11. A worthy supervisor will respect his employees' confidences.
12. Definite and clear-cut responsibilities should be assigned to each executive.
13. Responsibility should always be coupled with corresponding authority.
14. No change should be made in the scope or responsibilities of a position without a definite understanding to that effect on the part of all persons concerned.
15. No executive or employee, occupying a single position in the organization, should be subject to definite orders from more than one source.
16. Orders should never be given to subordinates over the head of a responsible executive. Rather than do this, the officer in question should be supplanted.
17. Criticisms of subordinates should, whoever possible, be made privately, and in no case should a subordinate be criticized in the presence of executives or employees of equal or lower rank.
18. No dispute or difference between executives or employees as to authority or responsibilities should be considered too trivial for prompt and careful adjudication.
19. Promotions, wage changes, and disciplinary action should always be approved by the executive immediately superior to the one directly responsible.
20. No executive or employee should ever be required, or expected, to be at the same time an assistant to, and critic of, another.
21. Any executive whose work is subject to regular inspection should, wherever practicable, be given the assistance and facilities necessary to enable him to maintain an independent check of the quality of his work.

MINI-TEXT IN SUPERVISION, ADMINISTRATION, MANAGEMENT, AND ORGANIZATION

I. Brief Highlights

Listed concisely and sequentially are major headings and important data in the field for quick recall and review.

A. Levels of Management
Any organization of some size has several levels of management. In terms of a ladder, the levels are:

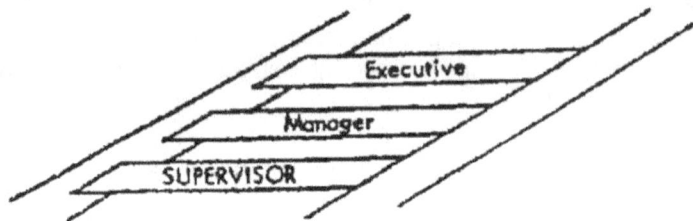

The first level is very important because it is the beginning point of management leadership.

B. What the Supervisor Must Learn
A supervisor must learn to:
1. Deal with people and their differences
2. Get the job done through people
3. Recognize the problems when they exist
4. Overcome obstacles to good performance
5. Evaluate the performance of people
6. Check his own performance in terms of accomplishment

C. A Definition of Supervisor
The term supervisor means any individual having authority, in the interests of the employer, to hire, transfer, suspend, lay-off, recall, promote, discharge, assign, reward, or discipline other employees or responsibility to direct them, or to adjust their grievances, or effectively to recommend such action, if, in connection with the foregoing, exercise of such authority is not of a merely routine or clerical nature but requires the use of independent judgment.

D. Elements of the Team Concept
What is involved in teamwork? The component parts are:
1. Members
2. A leader
3. Goals
4. Plans
5. Cooperation
6. Spirit

E. Principles of Organization
1. A team member must know what his job is.
2. Be sure that the nature and scope of a job are understood.
3. Authority and responsibility should be carefully spelled out.
4. A supervisor should be permitted to make the maximum number of decisions affecting his employees.
5. Employees should report to only one supervisor.
6. A supervisor should direct only as many employees as he can handle effectively.
7. An organization plan should be flexible.

8. Inspection and performance of work should be separate.
9. Organizational problems should receive immediate attention.
10. Assign work in line with ability and experience.

F. The Four Important Parts of Every Job
1. Inherent in every job is the *accountability* for results.
2. A second set of factors in every job is *responsibilities*.
3. Along with duties and responsibilities one must have the *authority* to act within certain limits without obtaining permission to proceed.
4. No job exists in a vacuum. The supervisor is surrounded by key *relationships*.

G. Principles of Delegation
Where work is delegated for the first time, the supervisor should think in terms of these questions:
1. Who is best qualified to do this?
2. Can an employee improve his abilities by doing this?
3. How long should an employee spend on this?
4. Are there any special problems for which he will need guidance?
5. How broad a delegation can I make?

H. Principles of Effective Communications
1. Determine the media.
2. To whom directed?
3. Identification and source authority.
4. Is communication understood?

I. Principles of Work Improvement
1. Most people usually do only the work which is assigned to them.
2. Workers are likely to fit assigned work into the time available to perform it.
3. A good workload usually stimulates output.
4. People usually do their best work when they know that results will be reviewed or inspected.
5. Employees usually feel that someone else is responsible for conditions of work, workplace layout, job methods, type of tools/equipment, and other such factors.
6. Employees are usually defensive about their job security.
7. Employees have natural resistance to change.
8. Employees can support or destroy a supervisor.
9. A supervisor usually earns the respect of his people through his personal example of diligence and efficiency.

J. Areas of Job Improvement
The areas of job improvement are quite numerous, but the most common ones which a supervisor can identify and utilize are:
1. Departmental layout
2. Flow of work
3. Workplace layout
4. Utilization of manpower
5. Work methods
6. Materials handling

7. Utilization
8. Motion economy

K. Seven Key Points in Making Improvements
1. Select the job to be improved
2. Study how it is being done now
3. Question the present method
4. Determine actions to be taken
5. Chart proposed method
6. Get approval and apply
7. Solicit worker participation

L. Corrective Techniques of Job Improvement
Specific Problems
1. Size of workload
2. Inability to meet schedules
3. Strain and fatigue
4. Improper use of men and skills
5. Waste, poor quality, unsafe conditions
6. Bottleneck conditions that hinder output
7. Poor utilization of equipment and machine
8. Efficiency and productivity of labor

General Improvement
1. Departmental layout
2. Flow of work
3. Work plan layout
4. Utilization of manpower
5. Work methods
6. Materials handling
7. Utilization of equipment
8. Motion economy

Corrective Techniques
1. Study with scale model
2. Flow chart study
3. Motion analysis
4. Comparison of units produced to standard allowance
5. Methods analysis
6. Flow chart and equipment study
7. Down time vs. running time
8. Motion analysis

M. A Planning Checklist
1. Objectives
2. Controls
3. Delegations
4. Communications
5. Resources
6. Manpower

7. Equipment
8. Supplies and materials
9. Utilization of time
10. Safety
11. Money
12. Work
13. Timing of improvements

N. Five Characteristics of Good Directions
In order to get results, directions must be:
1. Possible of accomplishment
2. Agreeable with worker interests
3. Related to mission
4. Planned and complete
5. Unmistakably clear

O. Types of Directions
1. Demands or direct orders
2. Requests
3. Suggestion or implication
4. volunteering

P. Controls
A typical listing of the overall areas in which the supervisor should establish controls might be:
1. Manpower
2. Materials
3. Quality of work
4. Quantity of work
5. Time
6. Space
7. Money
8. Methods

Q. Orienting the New Employee
1. Prepare for him
2. Welcome the new employee
3. Orientation for the job
4. Follow-up

R. Checklist for Orienting New Employees

		Yes	No
1.	Do you appreciate the feelings of new employees when they first report for work?	___	___
2.	Are you aware of the fact that the new employee must make a big adjustment to his job?	___	___
3.	Have you given him good reasons for liking the job and the organization?	___	___
4.	Have you prepared for his first day on the job?	___	___
5.	Did you welcome him cordially and make him feel needed?	___	___

	Yes	No

6. Did you establish rapport with him so that he feels free to talk and discuss matters with you? ___ ___
7. Did you explain his job to him and his relationship to you? ___ ___
8. Does he know that his work will be evaluated periodically on a basis that is fair and objective? ___ ___
9. Did you introduce him to his fellow workers in such a way that they are likely to accept him? ___ ___
10. Does he know what employee benefits he will receive? ___ ___
11. Does he understand the importance of being on the job and what to do if he must leave his duty station? ___ ___
12. Has he been impressed with the importance of accident prevention and safe practice? ___ ___
13. Does he generally know his way around the department? ___ ___
14. Is he under the guidance of a sponsor who will teach the right way of doing things? ___ ___
15. Do you plan to follow-up so that he will continue to adjust successfully to his job? ___ ___

S. Principles of Learning
1. Motivation
2. Demonstration or explanation
3. Practice

T. Causes of Poor Performance
1. Improper training for job
2. Wrong tools
3. Inadequate directions
4. Lack of supervisory follow-up
5. Poor communications
6. Lack of standards of performance
7. Wrong work habits
8. Low morale
9. Other

U. Four Major Steps in On-The-Job Instruction
1. Prepare the worker
2. Present the operation
3. Tryout performance
4. Follow-up

V. Employees Want Five Things
1. Security
2. Opportunity
3. Recognition
4. Inclusion
5. Expression

W. Some Don'ts in Regard to Praise
1. Don't praise a person for something he hasn't done.
2. Don't praise a person unless you can be sincere.
3. Don't be sparing in praise just because your superior withholds it from you.
4. Don't let too much time elapse between good performance and recognition of it

X. How to Gain Your Workers' Confidence
Methods of developing confidence include such things as:
1. Knowing the interests, habits, hobbies of employees
2. Admitting your own inadequacies
3. Sharing and telling of confidence in others
4. Supporting people when they are in trouble
5. Delegating matters that can be well handled
6. Being frank and straightforward about problems and working conditions
7. Encouraging others to bring their problems to you
8. Taking action on problems which impede worker progress

Y. Sources of Employee Problems
On-the-job causes might be such things as:
1. A feeling that favoritism is exercised in assignments
2. Assignment of overtime
3. An undue amount of supervision
4. Changing methods or systems
5. Stealing of ideas or trade secrets
6. Lack of interest in job
7. Threat of reduction in force
8. Ignorance or lack of communications
9. Poor equipment
10. Lack of knowing how supervisor feels toward employee
11. Shift assignments

Off-the-job problems might have to do with:
1. Health
2. Finances
3. Housing
4. Family

Z. The Supervisor's Key to Discipline
There are several key points about discipline which the supervisor should keep in mind:
1. Job discipline is one of the disciplines of life and is directed by the supervisor.
2. It is more important to correct an employee fault than to fix blame for it.
3. Employee performance is affected by problems both on the job and off.
4. Sudden or abrupt changes in behavior can be indications of important employee problems.
5. Problems should be dealt with as soon as possible after they are identified.
6. The attitude of the supervisor may have more to do with solving problems than the techniques of problem solving.
7. Correction of employee behavior should be resorted to only after the supervisor is sure that training or counseling will not be helpful.

8. Be sure to document your disciplinary actions.
9. Make sure that you are disciplining on the basis of facts rather than personal feelings.
10. Take each disciplinary step in order, being careful not to make snap judgments, or decisions based on impatience.

AA. Five Important Processes of Management
1. Planning
2. Organizing
3. Scheduling
4. Controlling
5. Motivating

BB. When the Supervisor Fails to Plan
1. Supervisor creates impression of not knowing his job
2. May lead to excessive overtime
3. Job runs itself—supervisor lacks control
4. Deadlines and appointments missed
5. Parts of the work go undone
6. Work interrupted by emergencies
7. Sets a bad example
8. Uneven workload creates peaks and valleys
9. Too much time on minor details at expense of more important tasks

CC. Fourteen General Principles of Management
1. Division of work
2. Authority and responsibility
3. Discipline
4. Unity of command
5. Unity of direction
6. Subordination of individual interest to general interest
7. Remuneration of personnel
8. Centralization
9. Scalar chain
10. Order
11. Equity
12. Stability of tenure of personnel
13. Initiative
14. Esprit de corps

DD. Change

Bringing about change is perhaps attempted more often, and yet less well understood, than anything else the supervisor does. How do people generally react to change? (People tend to resist change that is imposed upon them by other individuals or circumstances.

Change is characteristic of every situation. It is a part of every real endeavor where the efforts of people are concerned.

1. Why do people resist change?
   People may resist change because of:
   a. Fear of the unknown
   b. Implied criticism
   c. Unpleasant experiences in the past
   d. Fear of loss of status
   e. Threat to the ego
   f. Fear of loss of economic stability

2. How can we best overcome the resistance to change?
   In initiating change, take these steps:
   a. Get ready to sell
   b. Identify sources of help
   c. Anticipate objections
   d. Sell benefits
   e. Listen in depth
   f. Follow up

II. Brief Topical Summaries

   A. Who/What is the Supervisor?
      1. The supervisor is often called the "highest level employee and the lowest level manager."
      2. A supervisor is a member of both management and the work group. He acts as a bridge between the two.
      3. Most problems in supervision are in the area of human relations, or people problems.
      4. Employees expect: Respect, opportunity to learn and to advance, and a sense of belonging, and so forth.
      5. Supervisors are responsible for directing people and organizing work. Planning is of paramount importance.
      6. A position description is a set of duties and responsibilities inherent to a given position.
      7. It is important to keep the position description up-to-date and to provide each employee with his own copy.

   B. The Sociology of Work
      1. People are alike in many ways; however, each individual is unique.
      2. The supervisor is challenged in getting to know employee differences. Acquiring skills in evaluating individuals is an asset.
      3. Maintaining meaningful working relationships in the organization is of great importance.
      4. The supervisor has an obligation to help individuals to develop to their fullest potential.
      5. Job rotation on a planned basis helps to build versatility and to maintain interest and enthusiasm in work groups.
      6. Cross training (job rotation) provides backup skills.

7. The supervisor can help reduce tension by maintaining a sense of humor, providing guidance to employees, and by making reasonable and timely decisions. Employees respond favorably to working under reasonably predictable circumstances.
8. Change is characteristic of all managerial behavior. The supervisor must adjust to changes in procedures, new methods, technological changes, and to a number of new and sometimes challenging situations.
9. To overcome the natural tendency for people to resist change, the supervisor should become more skillful in initiating change.

C. Principles and Practices of Supervision
1. Employees should be required to answer to only one superior.
2. A supervisor can effectively direct only a limited number of employees, depending upon the complexity, variety, and proximity of the jobs involved.
3. The organizational chart presents the organization in graphic form. It reflects lines of authority and responsibility as well as interrelationships of units within the organization.
4. Distribution of work can be improved through an analysis using the "Work Distribution Chart."
5. The "Work Distribution Chart" reflects the division of work within a unit in understandable form.
6. When related tasks are given to an employee, he has a better chance of increasing his skills through training.
7. The individual who is given the responsibility for tasks must also be given the appropriate authority to insure adequate results.
8. The supervisor should delegate repetitive, routine work. Preparation of recurring reports, maintaining leave and attendance records are some examples.
9. Good discipline is essential to good task performance. Discipline is reflected in the actions of employees on the job in the absence of supervision.
10. Disciplinary action may have to be taken when the positive aspects of discipline have failed. Reprimand, warning, and suspension are examples of disciplinary action.
11. If a situation calls for a reprimand, be sure it is deserved and remember it is to be done in private.

D. Dynamic Leadership
1. A style is a personal method or manner of exerting influence.
2. Authoritarian leaders often see themselves as the source of power and authority.
3. The democratic leader often perceives the group as the source of authority and power.
4. Supervisors tend to do better when using the pattern of leadership that is most natural for them.
5. Social scientists suggest that the effective supervisor use the leadership style that best fits the problem or circumstances involved.
6. All four styles—telling, selling, consulting, joining—have their place. Using one does not preclude using the other at another time.

7. The theory X point of view assumes that the average person dislikes work, will avoid it whenever possible, and must be coerced to achieve organizational objectives.
8. The theory Y point of view assumes that the average person considers work to be a natural as play, and, when the individual is committed, he requires little supervision or direction to accomplish desired objectives.
9. The leader's basic assumptions concerning human behavior and human nature affect his actions, decisions, and other managerial practices.
10. Dissatisfaction among employees is often present, but difficult to isolate. The supervisor should seek to weaken dissatisfaction by keeping promises, being sincere and considerate, keeping employees informed, and so forth.
11. Constructive suggestions should be encouraged during the natural progress of the work.

E. Processes for Solving Problems
1. People find their daily tasks more meaningful and satisfying when they can improve them.
2. The causes of problems, or the key factors, are often hidden in the background. Ability to solve problems often involves the ability to isolate them from their backgrounds. There is some substance to the cliché that some persons "can't see the forest for the trees."
3. New procedures are often developed from old ones. Problems should be broken down into manageable parts. New ideas can be adapted from old one.
4. People think differently in problem-solving situations. Using a logical, patterned approach is often useful. One approach found to be useful includes these steps:
   a. Define the problem
   b. Establish objectives
   c. Get the facts
   d. Weigh and decide
   e. Take action
   f. Evaluate action

F. Training for Results
1. Participants respond best when they feel training is important to them.
2. The supervisor has responsibility for the training and development of those who report to him.
3. When training is delegated to others, great care must be exercised to insure the trainer has knowledge, aptitude, and interest for his work as a trainer.
4. Training (learning) of some type goes on continually. The most successful supervisor makes certain the learning contributes in a productive manner to operational goals.
5. New employees are particularly susceptible to training. Older employees facing new job situations require specific training, as well as having need for development and growth opportunities.
6. Training needs require continuous monitoring.
7. The training officer of an agency is a professional with a responsibility to assist supervisors in solving training problems.

8. Many of the self-development steps important to the supervisor's own growth are equally important to the development of peers and subordinates. Knowledge of these is important when the supervisor consults with others on development and growth opportunities.

G. Health, Safety, and Accident Prevention
1. Management-minded supervisors take appropriate measures to assist employees in maintaining health and in assuring safe practices in the work environment.
2. Effective safety training and practices help to avoid injury and accidents.
3. Safety should be a management goal. All infractions of safety which are observed should be corrected without exception.
4. Employees' safety attitude, training and instruction, provision of safe tools and equipment, supervision, and leadership are considered highly important factors which contribute to safety and which can be influenced directly by supervisors.
5. When accidents do occur, they should be investigated promptly for very important reasons, including the fact that information which is gained can be used to prevent accidents in the future.

H. Equal Employment Opportunity
1. The supervisor should endeavor to treat all employees fairly, without regard to religion, race, sex, or national origin.
2. Groups tend to reflect the attitude of the leader. Prejudice can be detected even in very subtle form. Supervisors must strive to create a feeling of mutual respect and confidence in every employee.
3. Complete utilization of all human resources is a national goal. Equitable consideration should be accorded women in the work force, minority-group members, the physically and mentally handicapped, and the older employee. The important question is: "Who can do the job?"
4. Training opportunities, recognition for performance, overtime assignments, promotional opportunities, and all other personnel actions are to be handled on an equitable basis.

I. Improving Communications
1. Communications is achieving understanding between the sender and the receiver of a message. It also means sharing information—the creation of understanding.
2. Communication is basic to all human activity. Words are means of conveying meanings; however, real meanings are in people.
3. There are very practical differences in the effectiveness of one-way, impersonal, and two-way communications. Words spoken face-to-face are better understood. Telephone conversations are effective, but lack the rapport of person-to-person exchanges. The whole person communicates.
4. Cooperation and communication in an organization go hand in hand. When there is a mutual respect between people, spelling out rules and procedures for communicating is unnecessary.
5. There are several barriers to effective communications. These include failure to listen with respect and understanding, lack of skill in feedback, and misinterpreting the meanings of words used by the speaker. It is also common

practice to listen to what we want to hear, and tune out things we do not want to hear.
6. Communication is management's chief problem. The supervisor should accept the challenge to communicate more effectively and to improve interagency and intra-agency communications.
7. The supervisor may often plan for and conduct meetings. The planning phase is critical and may determine the success or the failure of a meeting.
8. Speaking before groups usually requires extra effort. Stage fright may never disappear completely, but it can be controlled.

J. Self-Development
1. Every employee is responsible for his own self-development.
2. Toastmaster and toastmistress clubs offer opportunities to improve skills in oral communications.
3. Planning for one's own self-development is of vital importance. Supervisors know their own strengths and limitations better than anyone else.
4. Many opportunities are open to aid the supervisor in his developmental efforts, including job assignments; training opportunities, both governmental and non-governmental—to include universities and professional conferences and seminars.
5. Programmed instruction offers a means of studying at one's own rate.
6. Where difficulties may arise from a supervisor's being away from his work for training, he may participate in televised home study or correspondence courses to meet his self-development needs.

K. Teaching and Training
1. The Teaching Process
Teaching is encouraging and guiding the learning activities of students toward established goals. In most cases this process consists of five steps: preparation, presentation, summarization, evaluation, and application.

   a. Preparation
   Preparation is two-fold in nature; that of the supervisor and the employee. Preparation by the supervisor is absolutely essential to success. He must know what, when, where, how, and whom he will teach. Some of the factors that should be considered are:
   1) The objectives
   2) The materials needed
   3) The methods to be used
   4) Employee participation
   5) Employee interest
   6) Training aids
   7) Evaluation
   8) Summarization

   Employee preparation consists in preparing the employee to receive the material. Probably the most important single factor in the preparation of the employee is arousing and maintaining his interest. He must know the objectives of the training, why he is there, how the material can be used, and its importance to him.

b. Presentation
In presentation, have a carefully designed plan and follow it. The plan should be accurate and complete, yet flexible enough to meet situations as they arise. The method of presentation will be determined by the particular situation and objectives.

c. Summary
A summary should be made at the end of every training unit and program. In addition, there may be internal summaries depending on the nature of the material being taught. The important thing is that the trainee must always be able to understand how each part of the new material relates to the whole.

d. Application
The supervisor must arrange work so the employee will be given a chance to apply new knowledge or skills while the material is still clear in his mind and interest is high. The trainee does not really know whether he has learned the material until he has been given a chance to apply it. If the material is not applied, it loses most of its value.

e. Evaluation
The purpose of all training is to promote learning. To determine whether the training has been a success or failure, the supervisor must evaluate this learning.
In the broadest sense, evaluation includes all the devices, methods, skills, and techniques used by the supervisor to keep himself and the employees informed as to their progress toward the objectives they are pursuing. The extent to which the employee has mastered the knowledge, skills, and abilities, or changed his attitudes, as determined by the program objectives, is the extent to which instruction has succeeded or failed.
Evaluation should not be confined to the end of the lesson, day, or program but should be used continuously. We shall note later the way this relates to the rest of the teaching process.

2. Teaching Methods
A teaching method is a pattern of identifiable student and instructor activity used in presenting training material.
All supervisors are faced with the problem of deciding which method should be used at a given time.

a. Lecture
The lecture is direct oral presentation of material by the supervisor. The present trend is to place less emphasis on the trainer's activity and more on that of the trainee.

b. Discussion
Teaching by discussion or conference involves using questions and other techniques to arouse interest and focus attention upon certain areas, and by doing so creating a learning situation. This can be one of the most

valuable methods because it gives the employees an opportunity to express their ideas and pool their knowledge.

c. Demonstration
The demonstration is used to teach how something works or how to do something. It can be used to show a principle or what the results of a series of actions will be. A well-staged demonstration is particularly effective because it shows proper methods of performance in a realistic manner.

d. Performance
Performance is one of the most fundamental of all learning techniques or teaching methods. The trainee may be able to tell how a specific operation should be performed but he cannot be sure he knows how to perform the operation until he has done so.
As with all methods, there are certain advantages and disadvantages to each method.

e. Which Method to Use
Moreover, there are other methods and techniques of teaching. It is difficult to use any method without other methods entering into it. In any learning situation, a combination of methods is usually more effective than any one method alone.

Finally, evaluation must be integrated into the other aspects of the teaching-learning process.

It must be used in the motivation of the trainees; it must be used to assist in developing understanding during the training; and it must be related to employee application of the results of training.

This is distinctly the role of the supervisor.

BASIC FUNDAMENTALS OF BOOKKEEPING

CONTENTS

		Page
I.	INTRODUCTION	1
II.	REQUIREMENTS OF A GOOD RECORD SYSTEM	1
III.	IMPORTANT BOOKKEEPING RECORDS	2

    A. Bookkeeping Books — 2
    B. Financial Reports — 2
    C. The Balance Sheet — 3

        1. Assets — 3
            a. Current Assets — 4
            b. Fixed Assets — 4
            c. Other Assets — 5

        2. Liabilities — 5
            a. Current Liabilities — 5
            b. Long-Term Liabilities — 6

    D. The Income Statement — 6
        1. Sales — 7
        2. Cost of Goods Sold — 7
        3. Gross Margin — 7
        4. Net Profit — 8

IV.	OTHER RECORDS	9

    A. Daily Summary of Sales and Cash Receipts — 9
    R. Petty Cash and Charge Funds — 10
    C. Record of Cash Disbursement — 11
    D. Accounts Receivable Records — 12
    E. Property Records and Depreciation — 12
    F. Schedule of Insurance Coverage — 13

V.	CONCLUSION	13

BASIC FUNDAMENTALS OF BOOKKEEPING

I. INTRODUCTION

Why keep records? If you are a typical small-business man, your answer to this question is probably, "Because the Government requires it!" And if the question comes in the middle of a busy day, you may add a few heartfelt words about the amount of time you have to spend on records--just for the Government.

Is it "just for the Government," though? True, regulations of various governmental agencies have greatly increased the record-keeping requirements of business. But this may be a good thing for the small-business man, overburdened though he is.

Many small-business managers don't recognize their bookkeeping records for what they can really do. Their attitudes concerning these records are typified by one businessman who said, "Records only tell you what you have done in the past. It's too late to do anything about the past; I need to know what is going to happen in the future. "However, the past can tell us much about what may happen in the future; and, certainly we can profit in the future from knowledge of our past mistakes.

These same managers may recognize that records are necessary in filing their tax returns, or that a banker requires financial information before he will lend money, but often their appreciation of their bookkeeping systems ends at this point. However, there are many ways in which the use of such information can help an owner manage his business more easily and profitably.

The small-businessman is confronted with an endless array of problems and decisions every day. Sound decisions require an informed manager; and many management problems can be solved with the aid of the right bookkeeping information.

II. REQUIREMENTS OF A GOOD RECORD SYSTEM

Of course, to get information that is really valuable to you--to get the right information--requires a good bookkeeping system. What are the characteristics of a good system? You want one that is simple and easy to understand, reliable, accurate, consistent, and one that will get the information to you promptly.

A simple, well-organized system of records, regularly kept up, can actually be a timesaver--by bringing order out of disorder. Furthermore, competition is very strong in today's business areas. A businessman needs to know almost on a day-to-day basis where his business stands profit wise, which lines of merchandise or services are the most or the least profitable, what his working-capital needs are, and many other details. He can get this information with reasonable certainty only if he has a good recordkeeping system—one that gives him all the information he needs.

In setting up a recordkeeping system that is tailored to your business, you will probably need the professional help of a competent accountant. And you may want to retain the services of an accountant or bookkeeper to maintain these records. But it is your job to learn to interpret this information and to use it effectively.

One of the reasons that many managers have misgivings about keeping records is that they don't understand them or know how they can be used. The owner or manager of a small business may be an expert in his line of business; however, he generally does not have a background in keeping records. So he is usually confused. What we will try to do in this discussion is to highlight the "why and what of bookkeeping." In so-doing, we aim to eliminate that confusion.

III. IMPORTANT BOOKKEEPING RECORDS

Today's managers should be familiar with the following bookkeeping records:

- Journal
- Ledgers
- Balance sheet
- Income statement
- Funds flow statement

We will discuss each of them in turn. In addition, a brief discussion of other supporting records will be made.

A. Bookkeeping Books

The journal, which accountants call "the book of original entry," is a chronological record of all business transactions engaged in by the firm. It is simply a financial diary. The ledgers, or "books of account," are more specialized records used to classify the journal entries according to like elements. For example, there would be a separate ledger account for cash entries, another for all sales, and still others for items such as accounts receivable, inventory, and loans. All transactions are first entered in the journal, and then posted in the appropriate ledger. The journal and ledgers are of minor importance to the manager in making decisions, but they play a vital role for the accountant or bookkeeper because the more important accounting statements such as the balance sheet and the income statement are derived from the journal and ledger entries.

B. Financial Reports

The two principal financial reports in most businesses are the balance sheet and the income statement. Up to about 25 or 30 years ago, the balance sheet was generally considered to be the most important financial statement. Until that time, it was generally used only as a basis for the extension of credit and bank loans, and very little thought was given to the information it offered that might be important in „the operation and management of the business. Starting about 30 years ago, emphasis has gradually shifted to the income statement. Today the balance sheet and income statements are of equal importance, both to the accountant in financial reporting and to the manager faced with a multitude of administrative problems.

Essentially, the balance sheet shows what a business has, what it owes, and the investment of the owners in the business. It can be likened to a snapshot, showing the financial condition of the business *at a certain point in time*. The income statement, on the other hand, is a summary of business operations for a certain period--usually between two balance sheet dates. The income statement can be compared to a moving picture; it indicates the activity of a business *over a certain period of time*. In very general terms, the balance sheet tells you where you are, and the income statement tells you how you got there since the last time you had a balance sheet prepared.

Both the balance sheet and income statement can be long and complicated documents. Both accountants and management need some device that can highlight the critical financial information contained in these complex documents. Certain standard ratios or relationships between items on the financial statements have been developed that allow the interested parties to quickly determine important characteristics of the firm's activities. There are many relationships that might be important in a specific business that would not be as significant in another.

Other devices of the bookkeeper, such as funds flow statements, daily summaries of sales and cash receipts, the checkbook, account receivable records, property depreciation records, and insurance scheduling have also been found useful to management.

C. The Balance Sheet

As stated earlier, the balance sheet represents what a business has, what it owes, and the investment of the owners. The things of value that the business has or owns are called *assets*. The claims of creditors against these assets are called liabilities. The value of the assets over and above the *liabilities* can be justifiably called the owner's claim. This amount is usually called the owner's equity (or net worth).

This brings us to the *dual-aspect concept* of bookkeeping. The balance sheet is set up to portray two aspects of each entry or event recorded on it. For each thing of value, or asset, there is a claim against that asset. The recognition of this concept leads to the balance sheet formula: ASSETS = LIABILITIES + OWNER'S EQUITY. Let's take an example to clarify this concept. Suppose Joe Smith decides to start a business. He has $2,000 cash in the bank. He got this sum by investing $1,000 of his own money and by borrowing $1,000 from the bank. If he were to draw up a balance sheet at this time, he would have assets of $2 000 cash balanced against a liability claim of $1,000 and an owner's claim of $1,000. Using the balance sheet formula: $2,000 = $1,000 + $1,000. This formula means there will always be a balance between assets and claims against them. The balance sheet *always* balances unless there has been a clerical error.

The balance sheet is usually, constructed in a two-column format. The assets appear in the left hand column and the claims against the assets (the liabilities and owner's equity) are in the right hand column. Other formats are sometimes used; but, in any case, the balance sheet is-an itemized or detailed account of the basic formula: as sets = liabilities + owner's equity.

1. Assets

I have been speaking of assets belonging to the business. Of course, the business does not legally own anything unless it is organized as a corporation. But regardless of whether the business is organized as a proprietorship, a partnership, or a corporation, all business bookkeeping should be reckoned and accounted apart from the accounting of the personal funds and assets of, its owners.

Assets are typically classified into three categories:

- Current assets
- Fixed assets
- Other assets

a. Current Assets

For bookkeeping purposes, the term "current assets" is used to designate cash and other assets which can be converted to cash during the normal operating cycle of the business (usually one year). The distinction between current assets and noncurrent assets is important since lenders and others pay much attention to the total amount of current assets. The size of current assets has a significant relationship to the stability of the business because it represents, to some degree, the amount of cash that might be raised quickly to meet current obligations. Here are some of the major current asset items.

Cash consists of funds that are immediately available to use without restrictions. These funds are usually in the form of checking-account deposits in banks, cash-register money, and petty cash. Cash should be large enough to meet obligations that are immediately due.

Accounts, receivable are Arricnint8 'Owed to the company by its customers as a result of sales. Essentially, these accounts are the result of granting credit to customers. They may take the form of charge accounts where no interest or service charge is made, or they may be of an interest-bearing nature. In either case they are a drain on working capital. The more that is outstanding on accounts receivable, the less money that is available to meet current needs. The trick with accounts receivable is to keep them small enough so as not to endanger working capital, but large enough to keep from losing sales to credit-minded customers.

Inventory is defined as those items which are held for sale in the ordinary course of business, or which are to be consumed in the production of goods and services that are to be sold. Since accountants are conservative by nature, they include in inventory only items that are salable, and these items are valued at cost or market value, whichever is lower? Control of inventory and inventory expenses is one of management's most important jobs-particularly for retailers-- and good bookkeeping records in this area are particularly useful.

Prepaid expenses represent assets, paid for in advance, but whose usefulness will usually expire in a short time. A good example of this is prepaid insurance. A business pays for insurance protection in advance--usually three to five years in advance. The right to this protection is a thing of value--an asset--and the unused portion can be refunded or converted to cash.

b. Fixed Assets

"Fixed assets" are items owned by the business that have relatively long life. These assets are used in the production or sale of other goods and services. If they were held for resale, they would be classified as inventory, even though they might be long-lived assets.

Normally these assets are composed of land, buildings, and equipment. Some companies lump their fixed assets into one entry on their balance sheets, but you gain more information and can exercise more control over these assets if they are listed separately on the balance sheet. You may even want to list various types of equipment separately.

There is one other aspect of fixed-asset bookkeeping that we should discuss--and this is depreciation. Generally fixed assets-with the exception of land-depreciate, or decrease in value with the passing of time. That is, a building or piece of equipment that is five years old is not worth as much as it was when it was new. For a balance sheet to show the true value of these assets, it must reflect this loss in value. For both tax and other accounting purposes, the businessman is allowed to deduct this loss in value each year over the useful life of the assets, until, over a period of time, he has deducted the total cost of the asset. There are several accepted ways to calculate how much of an asset's value can be deducted for depreciation in a given year. Depreciation is allowed as an expense item on the income statement, and we will discuss this fact later.

c. Other Assets

"Other assets" is a miscellaneous category. It accounts for any investments of the firm in securities, such as stock in other private companies or government bonds. It also includes intangible assets such as goodwill, patents, and franchise costs. Items in the "other-assets" category have a longer life than current-asset items.

2. Liabilities

"Liabilities" are the amounts of money owed by the business to people other than the owners. They are claims against the company's total assets, although they are not claims against any specific asset, except in the cases of some mortgages and equipment liens. Essentially, liabilities are divided into two classes:

Current liabilities

Long-term Liabilities

a. Current Liabilities

The term "current liabilities" is used to describe those claims of outsiders on the business that will fall, due within one year. Here are some of the more important current-liabilities entries on the balance sheet:

Accounts payable represent the amounts owed to vendors, wholesalers, and other suppliers from whom the business has bought items on account. This includes any items of inventory, supply, or capital equipment which have been purchased on credit and for which payment is expected in less than one year. For example, a retail butcher purchased 500 pounds of meat for $250, a quantity of fish that cost $50, and a new air-conditioning unit for his store for $450. He bought all of these items on 60-day terms. His accounts payable were increased by $750. Of course, at the same time his inventory increased by $300 and his fixed assets rose by $450. If he had paid cash for these items, his accounts payable would not have been affected, but his cash account would have decreased by $750, thus keeping the accounting equation in balance.

Short-term loans, which are sometimes called notes payable, are loans from individuals, banks, or other lending institutions which fall due within a year. Also included in this category is the portion of any long-term debt that will come due within a year.

Accrued expenses are obligations which the company has incurred, but for 'which there has been no formal bill or invoice as yet. An example of this is accrued taxes. The owner knows the business has the obligation to pay taxes; and they are accruing or accumulating each day. The fact that the taxes do not have to be paid until a later date does not diminish the obligation. Another example of accrued expenses is wages. Although wages are paid weekly or monthly, they are being earned hourly or daily and constitute a valid claim against the company. An accurate balance sheet will reflect these obligations.

b. Long-Term Liabilities

Claims of outsiders on the business that do not come due within one year are called "long-term liabilities" or, simply, "other liabilities." Included in this category are bonded indebtedness, mortgages, and long-term loans from individuals, banks, and others from whom the business may borrow money, such as the SBA. As was stated before, any part of a long-term debt that falls due within one year from the date of the balance sheet would be recorded as part of the current liabilities of the business.

Owner's Equity

The owner's equity section of the balance sheet is located on the right-hand side underneath the listing of the liabilities. It shows the claims of the owners on the company. Essentially, this is a balancing figure--that is, the owners get what's left of the assets after the liability claims have been recognized. This is an obvious definition, if you will remember the balance sheet formula. Transposing the formula as we learned it a few minutes ago, it becomes Assets - Liabilities = Owner's Equity. In the case where the business is a sole proprietorship, it is customary to show owner's equity as one entry with no distinction being made between the owner's initial investment and the accumulated retained earnings of the business. However, in the case of an incorporated business, there are entries for stockholders' claims as well as for earnings that have been accumulated and retained in the business. Of course, if the business has been consistently operating at a loss, the proprietor's claim may be less than his initial investment. And, in the case of a corporation, the balancing account could be operating deficit rather than retained earnings.

If we put together the entries we have been talking about, we have a complete balance sheet. There is a lot of information in this statement. It tells you just what you have and where it is. It also tells you what you owe. You need this information to help you decide what actions you should take in running your business. If you need to borrow money, the banker or anyone else from whom you borrow will want to look at your balance sheet.

D. THE INCOME STATEMENT

In recent years the income statement has become as important as the balance sheet as a financial and management record. It is also called the profit and loss statement, or simply the P and L statement. This financial record summarizes the activities of the company over a period of time, listing those that can be expressed in dollars. That is, it reports the revenues of the company and the expenses incurred in obtaining the revenues, and it shows the profit or loss resulting from these activities. The income statement complements the balance sheet. While balance sheet analysis shows the change in position of the company at the end of accounting periods, the income statement shows how the change took place during the accounting period. Both reports 'are necessary for a full understanding of the operation of the business.

The income statement for particular company should be tailored to fit the activities of that company, and there is no rigid format that must be followed in constructing this report. But the following categories are found in most income statements.

1. Sales

The major activity of most businesses is the sales of products and services, and the bulk of revenue comes from sales. In recording sales, the figure used is net sales-that is, sales after discounts, allowances, and returned goods have been accounted for.

2. Cost of Goods Sold

Another important item, in calculating profit or loss, is the cost of the goods that the company has sold. This item is difficult to calculate accurately. Since the goods sold come from inventory, and since the company may have bought parts of its inventory at several prices, it is hard to determine exactly what is the cost of the particular part of the inventory that was sold. In large companies, and particularly in companies using cost accounting, there are some rather complicated methods of determining "cost of goods sold, " but they are beyond the scope of this presentation. However, there is a simple, generally accepted way of calculating cost of goods sold. In this method you simply add the net amount of purchases during the accounting period to your beginning inventory, and subtract from this your ending inventory. The result can be considered cost-of-goods sold.

3. Gross Margin

The difference between sales and cost of goods sold is called the "gross margin" or gross profit. This item is often expressed as a percentage of sales, as well as in dollar figures. The percentage gross margin is a very significant figure because it indicates what the average markup is on the merchandise sold. So, if a manager knows his expenses as a percentage of sales, he can calculate the mark up necessary to obtain the gross margin he needs for a profitable operation. It is surprising how many small-business men do not know what basis to use in setting markups. In fact, with the various, allowances, discounts, and markdowns that a business may offer, many managers do not know what their markup actually is. The gross margin calculation on the income statement can help the manager with this problem.

There are other costs of running a business besides the cost of the goods sold. When you use the simple method of determining costs of goods sold, these costs are called "expenses."

For example, here are some typical expenses: salaries and wages, utilities, depreciation, interest, administrative expenses, supplies, bad debts, advertising, and taxes--Federal, State, and local. These are typical expenses, but there are many other kinds of expenses that may be experienced by other businesses. For example, we have shown in the Blank Company's balance sheet that he owns his own land and building--with a mortgage, of course. These accounts for part of his depreciation and interest expenses, but for a company that rents its quarters, rent would appear as the expense item. Other common expenses are traveling expense, commissions, and advertising.

Most of these expense items are self-explanatory, but there are a few that merit further comment. For one thing, the salary or draw of the owner should be recorded among the expenses--either as a part of salaries and wages or as part of administrative expenses. To exclude the owner's compensation from expenses distorts the actual profitability of the business. And, if the company is incorporated, it would reduce the allowable tax deductions of the business. Of course, for tax purposes, the owner's salary or draw in a proprietorship or partnership is considered as part of the net profit.

We discussed depreciation when we examined the balance sheet, and we mentioned that it was an item of expense. Although no money is actually paid out for depreciation, it is a real expense because it represents reduction in the value of the assets.

The most important thing about expenses is to be sure to include all of the expenses that the business incurs. This not only helps the owner get a more accurate picture of his operation but it allows him to take full advantage of the tax deductions that legitimate expenses offer.

4. Net Profit

In a typical company when expenses are subtracted from gross margin, the remainder is profit. However, if the business receives revenue from sources other than sales, such as rents, dividends on securities held by the company, or interest on money loaned by the company, it is added to profit at this point. For bookkeeping purposes, the resulting profit is labeled "profit before taxes." This is the figure from which Federal income taxes are figured. If the business is a proprietorship, the profit is taxed as part of the owner's income. If the business is a corporation, the profits may be taxed on the basis of the corporate income tax schedule. When income taxes have been accounted for, the resultant entry is called "net profit after taxes," or simply "net profit." This is usually the final entry on the income statement.

Another financial record which managers can use to advantage is the funds flow statement. This statement is also called statement of sources and uses of funds and sometimes the "where got--where gone" statement. Whatever you call it, a record of sources and uses of past funds is useful to the manager. He can use it to evaluate past performance, and as a guide in determining future uses and sources of money.

When we speak of "funds" we do not necessarily mean actual "dollars" or "cash." Although accounting records are all written in monetary terms, they do not always involve an exchange of money. Many times in business transactions, it is credit rather than dollars that changes hands. Therefore, when we speak of funds flow, we are speaking of exchanges of *economic values* rather than merely the physical flow of dollars.

Basically, funds are used to: increase assets and reduce liabilities. They are also sometimes used to reduce owner's equity. An example of this would be the use of company funds to buy up outstanding stock or to buy out a partner. Where do funds come from? The three basic sources of funds are a reduction in assets, increases in liabilities, and increased owner's equity. All balance sheet items can be affected by the obtaining and spending of company fund's.

To examine the construction and use of a funds flow statement, let's take another look at the Blank Company. Here we show comparative balance sheets for two one-year periods. For the sake of simplicity, we have included only selected items from the balance sheets for analysis. Notice that the company gained funds by:

reducing cash $300,

increasing accounts payable $400,

putting $500 more owner's equity in the business, and

plowing back $800 of the profit into the business.

These funds were used to:

increase accounts receivable $300,
increase inventory $200,

buy $500 worth of equipment, and

pay off $1,000 worth of long-term debt.

This funds flow statement has indicated to Mr. Blank where he has gotten his funds and how he has spent them. He can analyze these figures in the light of his plans and objectives and take appropriate action.

For example, if Mr. Blank wants to answer the question "Should I buy new capital equipment?" a look at his funds flow statement would show him his previous sources of funds, and it would give him a clue as to whether he could obtain funds for any new equipment.

IV. OTHER RECORDS

Up to this point, we have been talking about the basic types of bookkeeping records. In addition, we have discussed the two basic financial statements of a business: the balance sheet and the profit and loss statement. Now let us give our attention briefly to some other records which are very helpful to running a business successfully.

One element that appears on the balance sheet which I believe we can agree is important is cash. Because it is the lifeblood of all business, cash should be controlled and safeguarded at all times. The daily summary of sales and cash receipts and the checkbook are used by many manager s of small businesses to help provide that control.

A. Daily Summary of Sales and Cash. Receipts

Not all businesses summarize their daily transactions. However, a daily summary of sales and cash receipts is a very useful tool for checking how your business is doing on a day-to-day basis. At the close of each day's business, the actual cash on hand is counted and "balanced" against the total of the receipts recorded for the day. This balancing is done by means of the Daily Summary of Sales and Cash Receipts. This is a recording of every cash 'receipt and every charge sale, whether you use a cash register or sales checks or both. If you have more than one cash register, a daily summary should be prepared for each; the individual cash-register summaries can then be combined into one overall summary for convenience in handling.

In the daily summary form used for purposes of illustration, (see Handout), the first section, "Cash Receipts," records the total of all cash taken in during the day from whatever source. This is the cash that must be accounted for over and above, the amount in the change and/ or petty cash funds. We shall touch upon these two funds later. The three components of cash receipts are (1) cash sales, (2) collections on accounts, and (3) miscellaneous receipts.

The daily total of cash sales is obtained from a cash-register tape reading or, if no cash register is used, by totaling the cash-sales checks.

For collections on accounts, an individual record of each customer payment on account should be kept, whether or not these collections are rung up on a cash register. The amount to be entered on the daily summary is obtained by totaling these individual records.

Miscellaneous receipts are daily cash transactions that cannot be classified as sales or collections. They might include refunds from suppliers for overpayment, advertising rebates or allowances, . collections of rent from sub-leases or concessions, etc. Like collections on account, a sales check or memo should be made out each time such cash is taken in.

The total of daily cash receipts to be accounted for on the daily summary is obtained by adding cash sales, collections on account, and miscellaneous receipts.

The second section, "Cash on Hand," of a daily summary is a count of the cash actually on hand plus the cash that is represented by petty cash slips. The daily summary provides for counts of your total coins, bills, and checks as well as the amount expended for petty cash. The latter is determined by adding the amounts on the individual petty cash slips. By totaling all four of these counts, you obtain the total cash accounted for. To determine the amount of your daily cash deposit, you deduct from the "total cash accounted for" the total of the petty cash and change funds.

Cash to be deposited on the daily summary should always equal the total receipts to be accounted for minus the fixed amount of your petty cash and change funds. If it does not, all the work in preparing the daily summary should be carefully checked. Obviously, an error in giving change, in ringing up a sale, or neglecting to do so, will result in a cash shortage or overage. The daily summary provides spaces for such errors so that the proper entries can be made in your bookkeeping records. The last section of your daily summary, "Sales," records the total daily sales broken down into (1) cash sales and (2) charge sales.

As soon as possible after the daily summary has been completed, all cash for deposit should be taken to the bank. A duplicate deposit slip, stamped by the bank, should be kept with the daily summary as evidence that the deposit was made.

B. Petty Cash and Charge Funds

The record of, daily, sales and cash. Receipts which we have just described. is designed. on the assumption that a petty cash fund and a change cash fund, or a combination change and petty cash fund, are used. All businesses, small and large, have day-to-day expenses that are so small they do not warrant the drawing of a check. Good management practice calls for careful control of such expenses. The petty cash fund provides such control. It is a sum of money which is obtained by drawing a check to provide several days, a week's, or a month's need of cash for small purchases. The type of business will determine the amount of the petty cash fund.

Each time a payment is made from the petty cash, a slip should be made out. If an invoice or receipt is available, it should be attached to the petty-cash slip. The slips and the money ordinarily, but not necessarily, are kept separate from other currency in your cash till, drawer, or register. At all times, the total of unspent petty cash and petty cash slips should equal the fixed amount of the fund. When the total of the slips approaches the fixed amount of the petty cash fund, a check is drawn for the total amount of the slips. The money from this check is used to bring the fund back to its fixed amount.

In addition to a petty cash fund, some businesses that receive cash in over-the-counter transactions have a change fund. The amount needed for making change varies with the size and type of business, and, in some cases, with the days of the week. Control of the money in your change fund will be made-easier, however, if you set a fixed amount large enough to meet all the ordinary change-making needs of your business. Each day, when the day's receipts are balanced and prepared for a bank deposit, you will retain bills and coins totaling the fixed amount of the fund for use the following day. Since you had that amount on hand before you made the day's first sale, the entire amount of the day's receipts will still be available for your bank deposit.

In some cases, the petty cash fund is kept in a petty cash box or safe, apart from the change fund. However, the same fund can serve for both petty cash and change. For example, if you decide that you need $50 for making change and $25 for petty cash, one $75 fund can be used. Whenever, in balancing the day's operations, you see that the petty cash slips total more than $25, you can write a petty cash check for the amount of the slips.

C. Record of Cash Disbursement

To safeguard your cash, it is recommended that all receipts be deposited in a bank account and that all disbursements, except those made from the petty cash fund, are made by drawing a check on that account. Your bank account should be used exclusively for business transactions. If your business is typical, you will have to write checks for merchandise purchases, employee's salaries, rent, utilities, payroll taxes, petty cash, and various other expenses. Your check stubs will serve as a record of cash disbursements.

The checkbook stub should contain all the details of the disbursement including the date, payee, amount and purpose of the payment. In addition, a running balance of the amount you have in your bank account should be maintained by subtracting the amount of each check from the existing balance after the previous check was drawn. If the checks of your checkbook are prenumbered, it is important to mark plainly in the stub when a check is voided for one reason or another.

Each check should have some sort of written document to support it--an invoice, petty-cash voucher, payroll summary and so on. Supporting documents should be approved by you or someone you have authorized before a check is drawn. They should be marked paid and filed after the check is drawn.

Periodically, your bank will send you a statement of your account and return cancelled checks for which money has been withdrawn from your account. It is important that you reconcile your records with those of the bank. This means that the balances in your checkbook and on the bank statement should agree. Uncashed checks must be deducted from your checkbook balance and deposits not recorded on the bank statement must be added to its balance in order to get both balances to agree.

D. Accounts Receivable Records

If you extend credit to your customers, you must keep an accurate account of your credit sales not only in total as you have done on the daily summary but also by the amount that each individual customer owes you. Moreover, you must be systematic about billings and collections. This is important. It results in better relations with your charge customers and in fewer losses from bad debts.

The simplest method of handling accounts receivable--other than just keeping a file of sales-slip carbons--is to have an account sheet for each credit customer. Charge sales and payments on charge sales are posted to each customer sheet. Monthly billing to each of your charge customers should be made from their individual account sheets.

At least two or three times a year, your accounts receivable should be aged. You do this by posting each customer's account and his unpaid charges in columns according to age. These columns are labeled: not due; 1 to 30 days past due; 31 to 60 days past due; 61 to 90 days past due; etc. This analysis will indicate those customers who are not complying with your credit terms.

E. Property Records and Depreciation

In every type of business, it is necessary to purchase property and equipment from time to time. This property usually will last for several years, so it would be unrealistic to show the total amount of the purchase as an expense in any one year. Therefore, when this property is set up in the books as an asset, records must be kept to decrease its value over its life. This decrease is known as depreciation. I have mentioned this before during this talk. The amount of the decrease in value in one year, that is, the depreciation, is charged as an expense for the year.

I am talking about this expense, particularly, because no cash is paid out for it. It is a non-cash, not-out-of-pocket expense. You don't have to hand over actual money at the end of the month.

Records should be kept of this because, otherwise, there is a danger that this expense will be overlooked. Yet it is impossible to figure true profit or loss without considering it. When you deduct the depreciation expense from your firm's income, you reduce your tax liabilities. When you put this depreciation expense into a depreciation allowance account, you are keeping score on your "debt" to depreciation.

In a barber shop, to take a simple example, depreciation of its chairs, dryers, and clippers at the end of the year amounts to $136. You deduct this $136 from the shop's income, in this case, to pay the debt credited to your depreciation allowance account. Since this equipment has the same depreciation value each year, the depreciation allowance account at the end of 3 years will show that a total of $408 worth of equipment has been used up. The books of the barbershop therefore show an expense of $408 which actually has not been spent. It is in the business to replace the depreciated equipment. If replacement will not take place in the immediate future, the money can be used in inventory, or in some other way to generate more sales or profits.

How you handle this money depends on many things. You can set it aside at a low interest rate and have that much less operating money. Or you can put it to work in your business where it will help to keep your finances healthy.

Remember, however, that you must be prepared financially when it is time to buy replacement equipment. A depreciation allowance account on your books can help to keep you aware of this. It helps you keep score on how much depreciation or replacement money you are using in your business.

Keeping score with a depreciation allowance account helps you to know when you need to convert some of your assets into replacement cash. If, for example, you know on January 1 that Your delivery truck will be totally depreciated by June 30, you can review the situation objectively. You can decide whether you ought to use the truck longer or replace it. If you decide to replace it, then you can plan to accumulate the cash, and time the purchase in order to make the best deal.

F. Schedule of Insurance Coverage

The schedule of insurance coverage is prepared to indicate the type of coverage and the amount presently in force. This schedule should list all the insurance carried by your business-- fire and extended coverage, theft, liability, life, business interruption and so forth.

This schedule should be prepared to present the following: name of insurance company, annual premium, expiration date, type of coverage, amount of coverage, asset insured, and estimated current value of asset insured.

An analysis of this schedule should indicate the adequacy of insurance coverage. A review of this schedule with your insurance agent is suggested.

V. CONCLUSION

During the brief time allotted to this subject of the basic fundamentals of bookkeeping, we have just scratched its surface. What we have tried to do is to inform you, as small-business managers, of the importance of good records. We have described the components of the important records that you must have if you are going to manage your business efficiently and profitably. In addition, we have brought to your attention some of the subsidiary records that will aid you in managing your business.

There are other records such as breakeven charts, budgets, cost accounting systems, to mention a few, which can also benefit the progressive manager. However, we do not have the time even to give you the highlights of those management tools. Your accountant can assist you in learning to understand and use them. Moreover, he can help you to develop and use the records we have discussed. For further information about them, you also can read the publications of the Small Business Administration, some of which are available to you free of charge.

By reading and using the accounting advice available to you, you can make sure that you have the right records to improve your managing skill and thereby increase your profits.

www.ingramcontent.com/pod-product-compliance
Lightning Source LLC
Chambersburg PA
CBHW082040300426
44117CB00015B/2549